Color Test Page

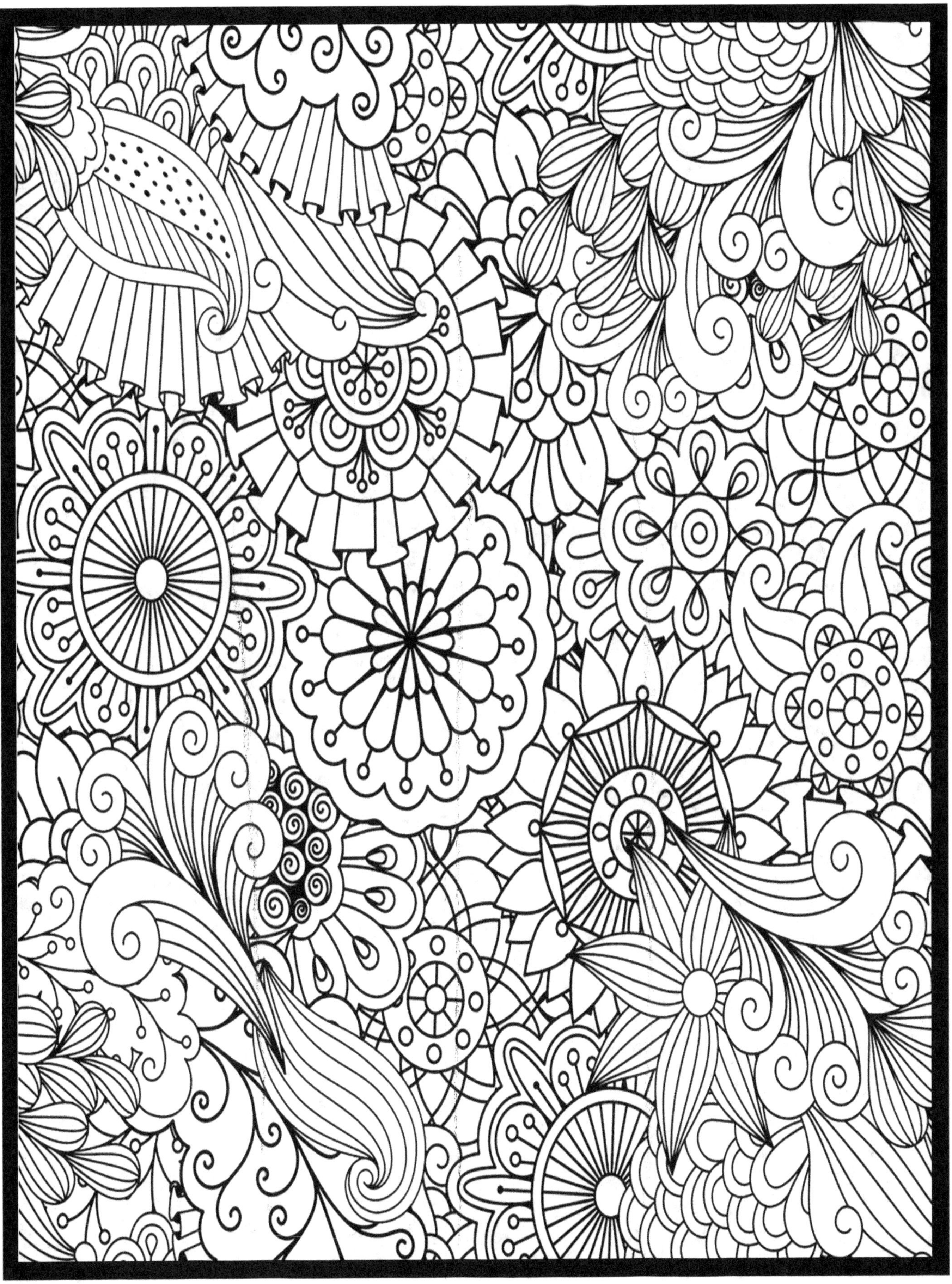

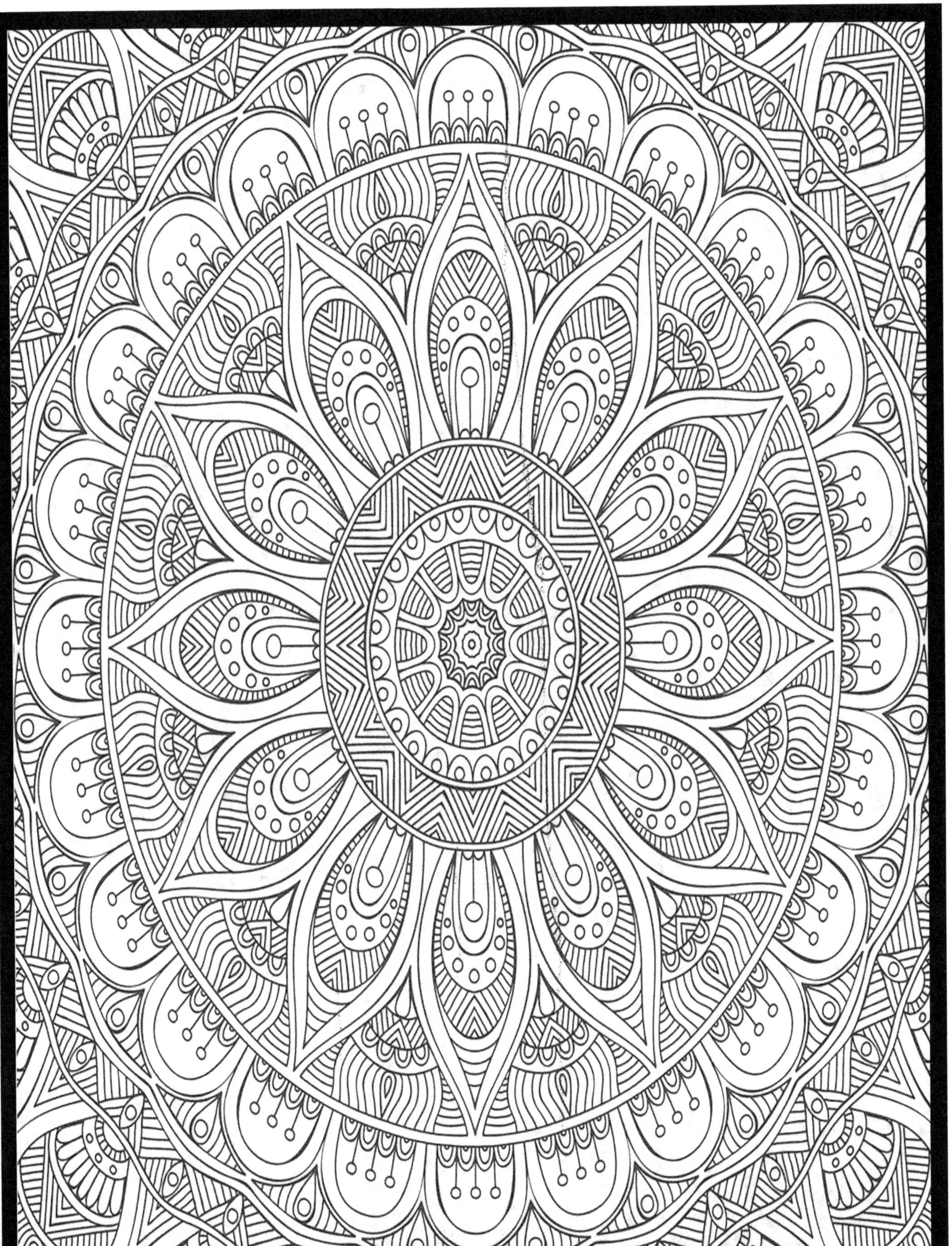

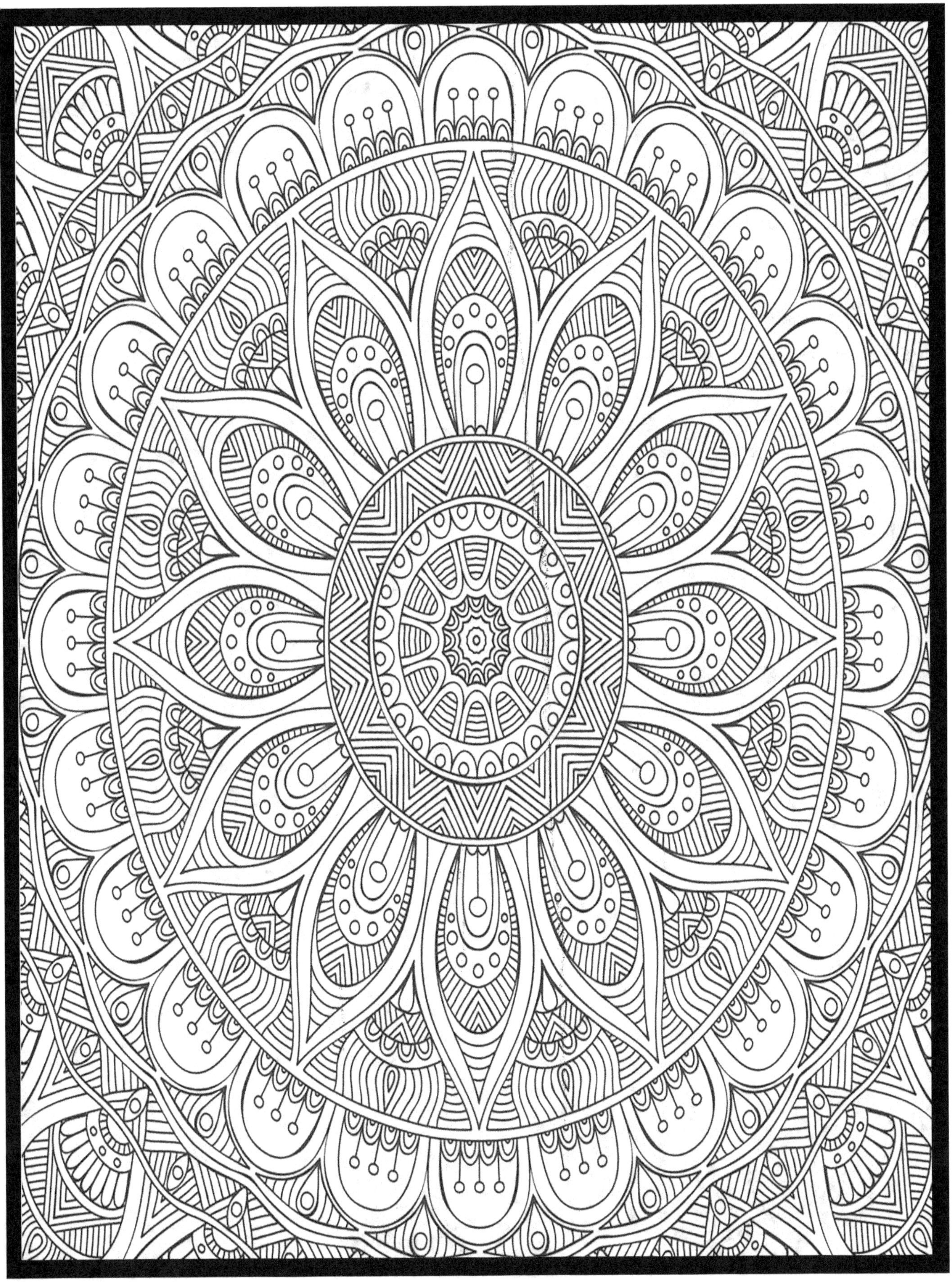

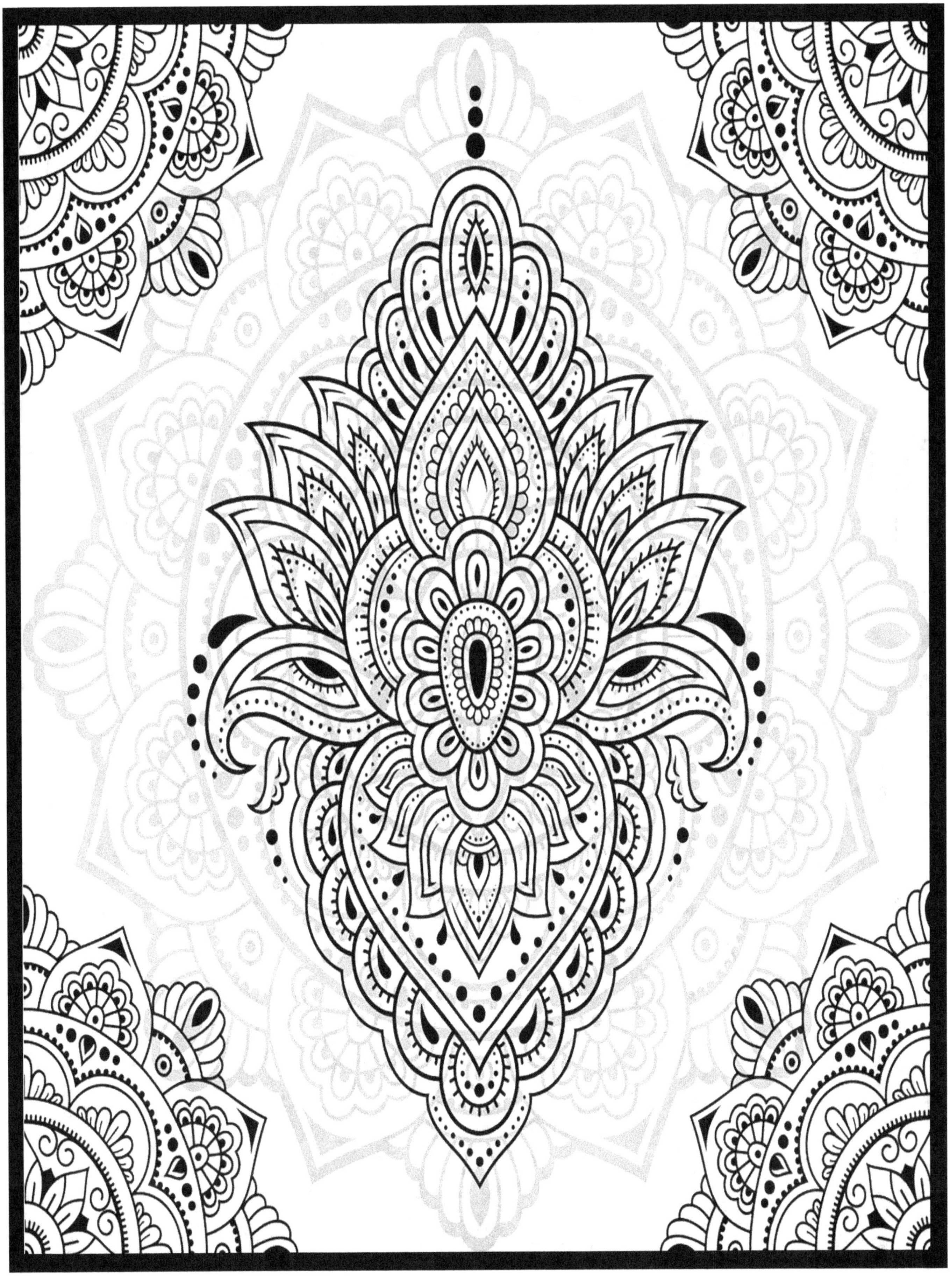

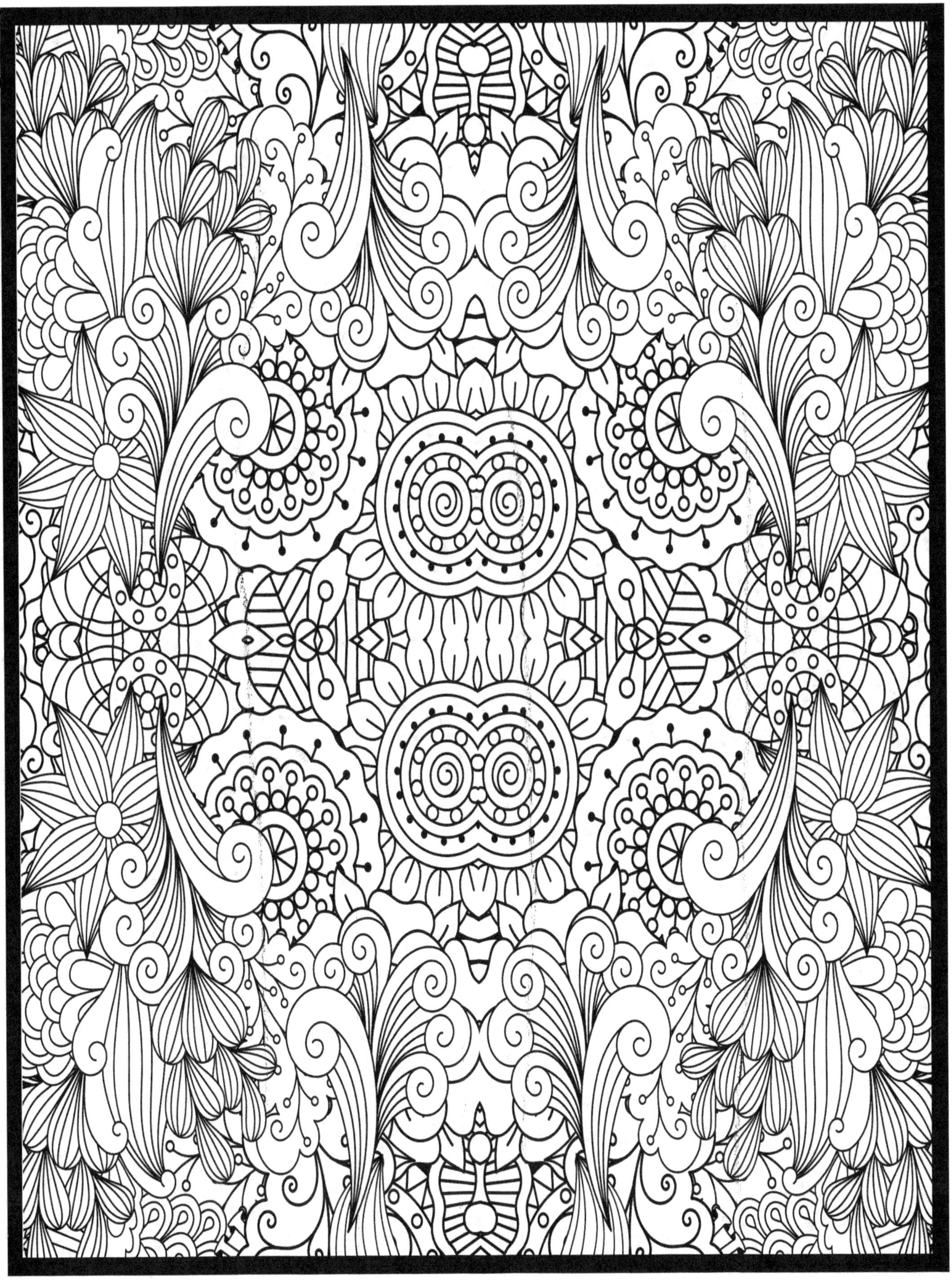

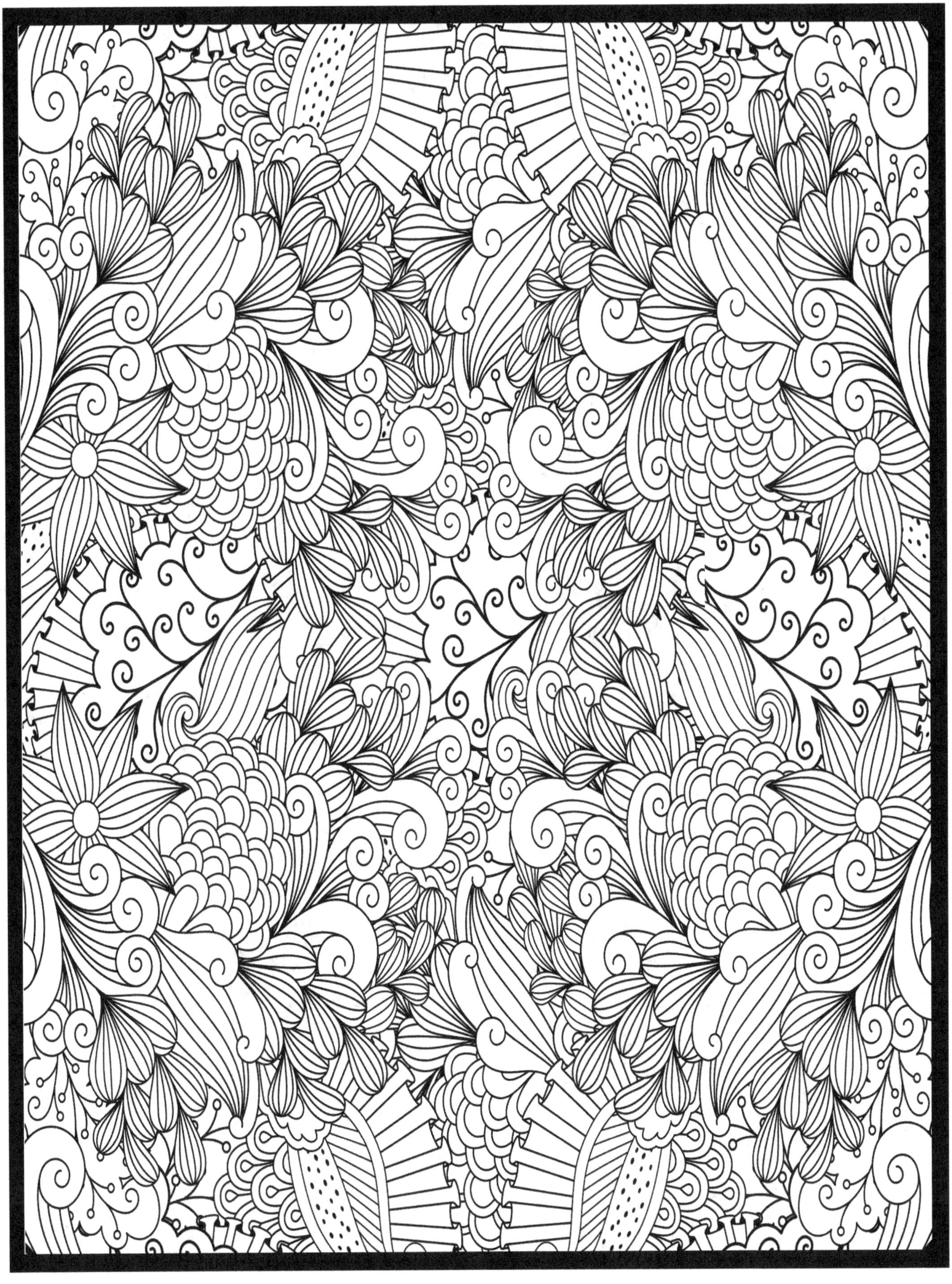

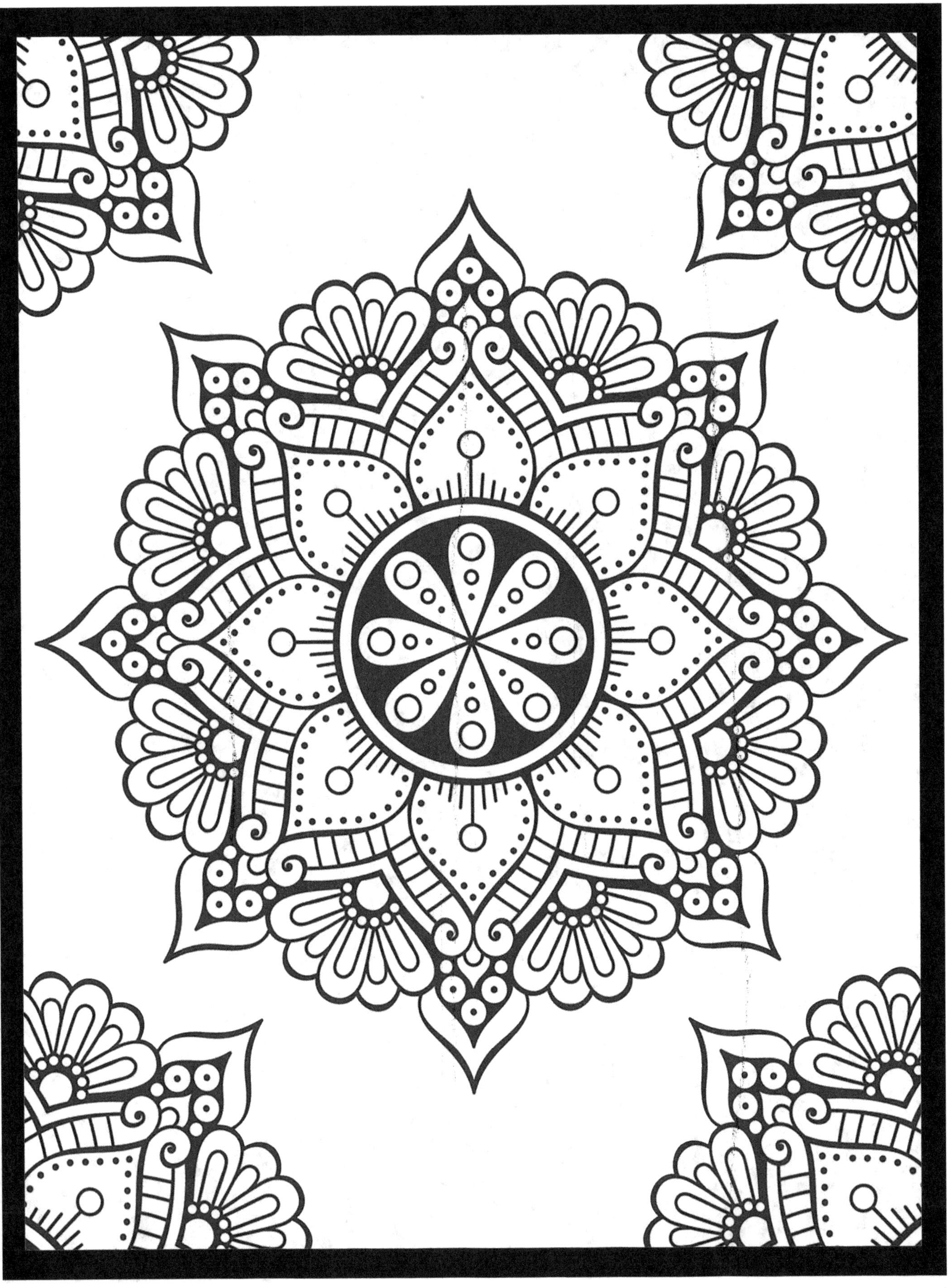

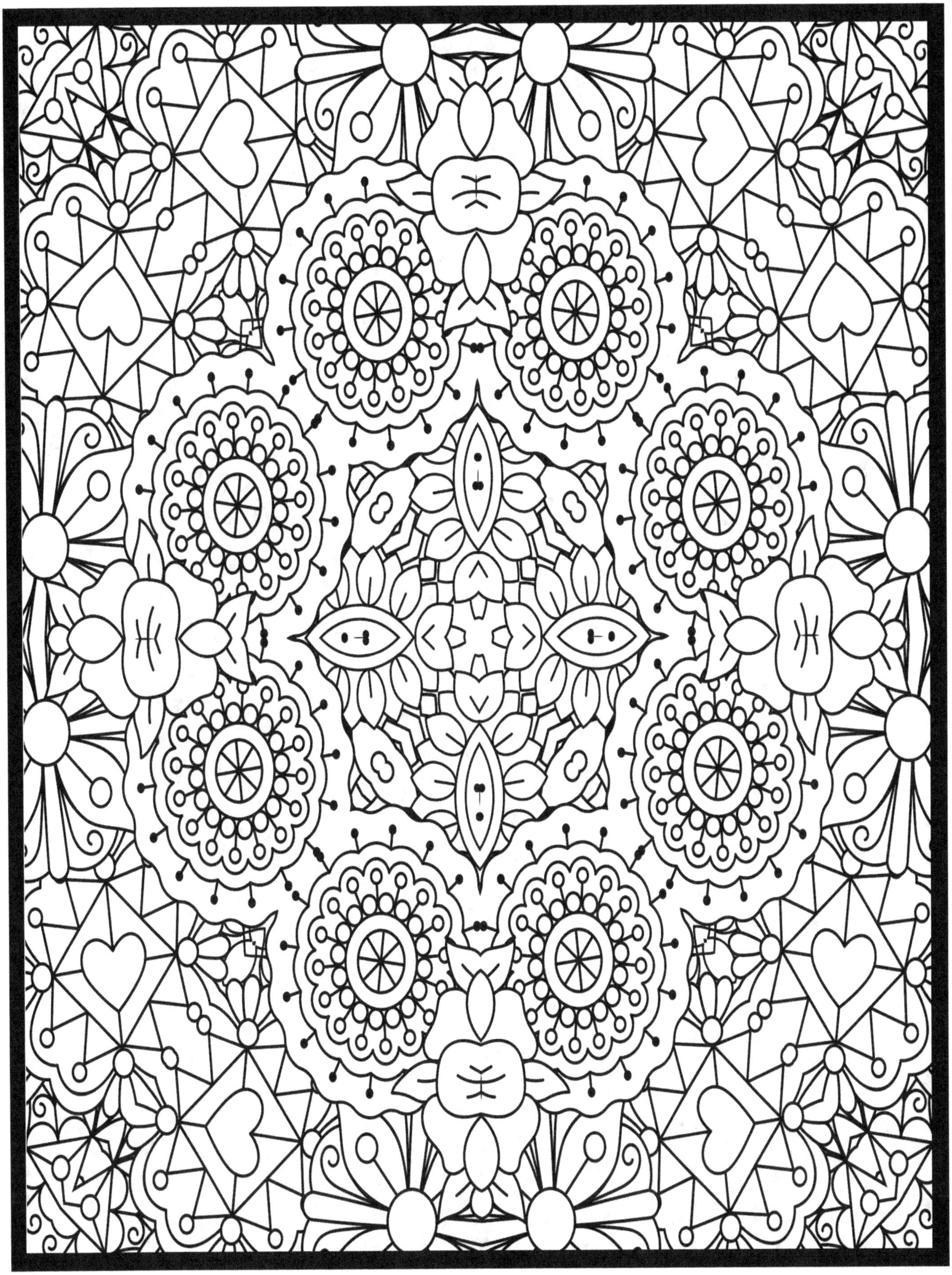

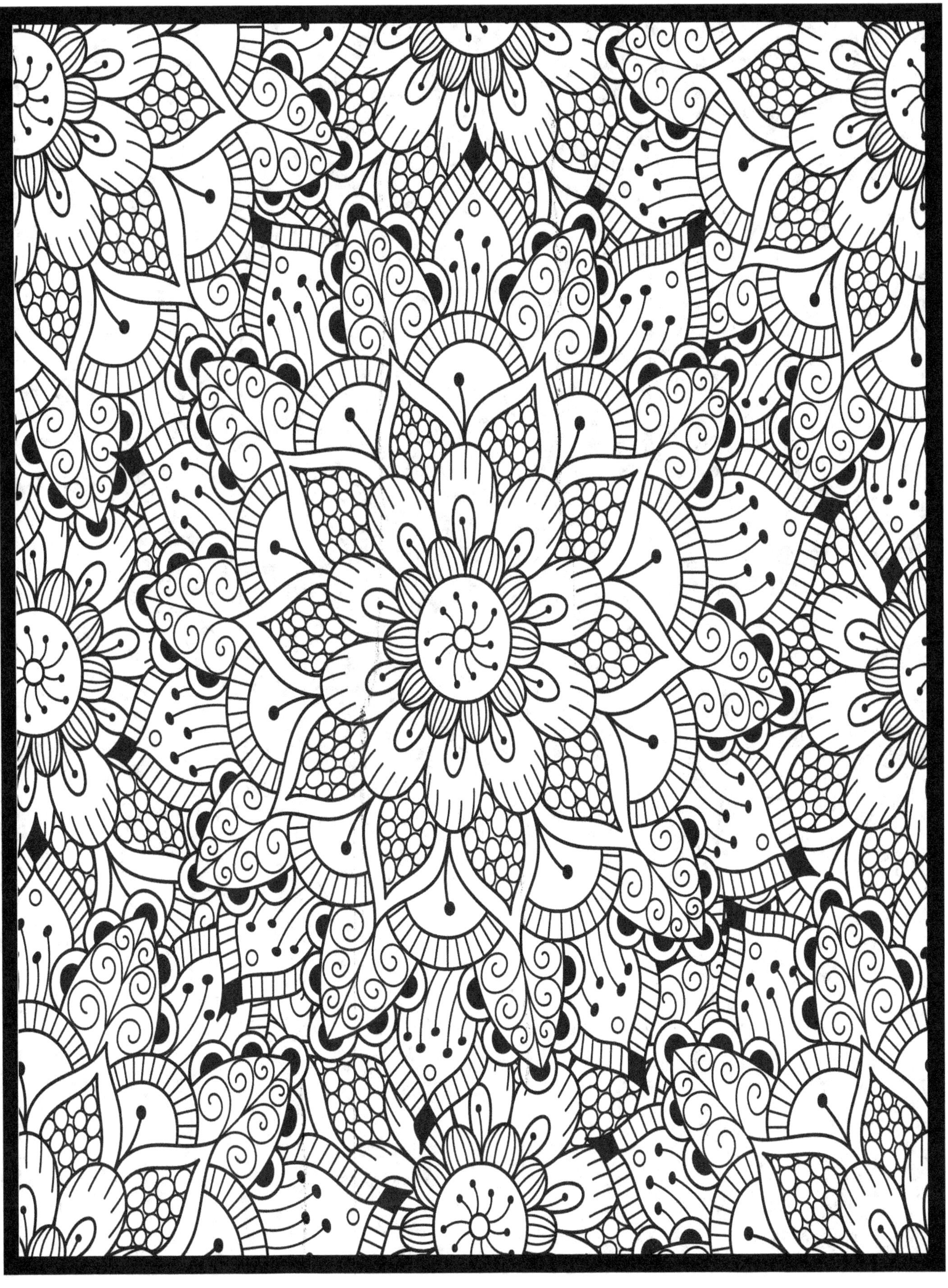

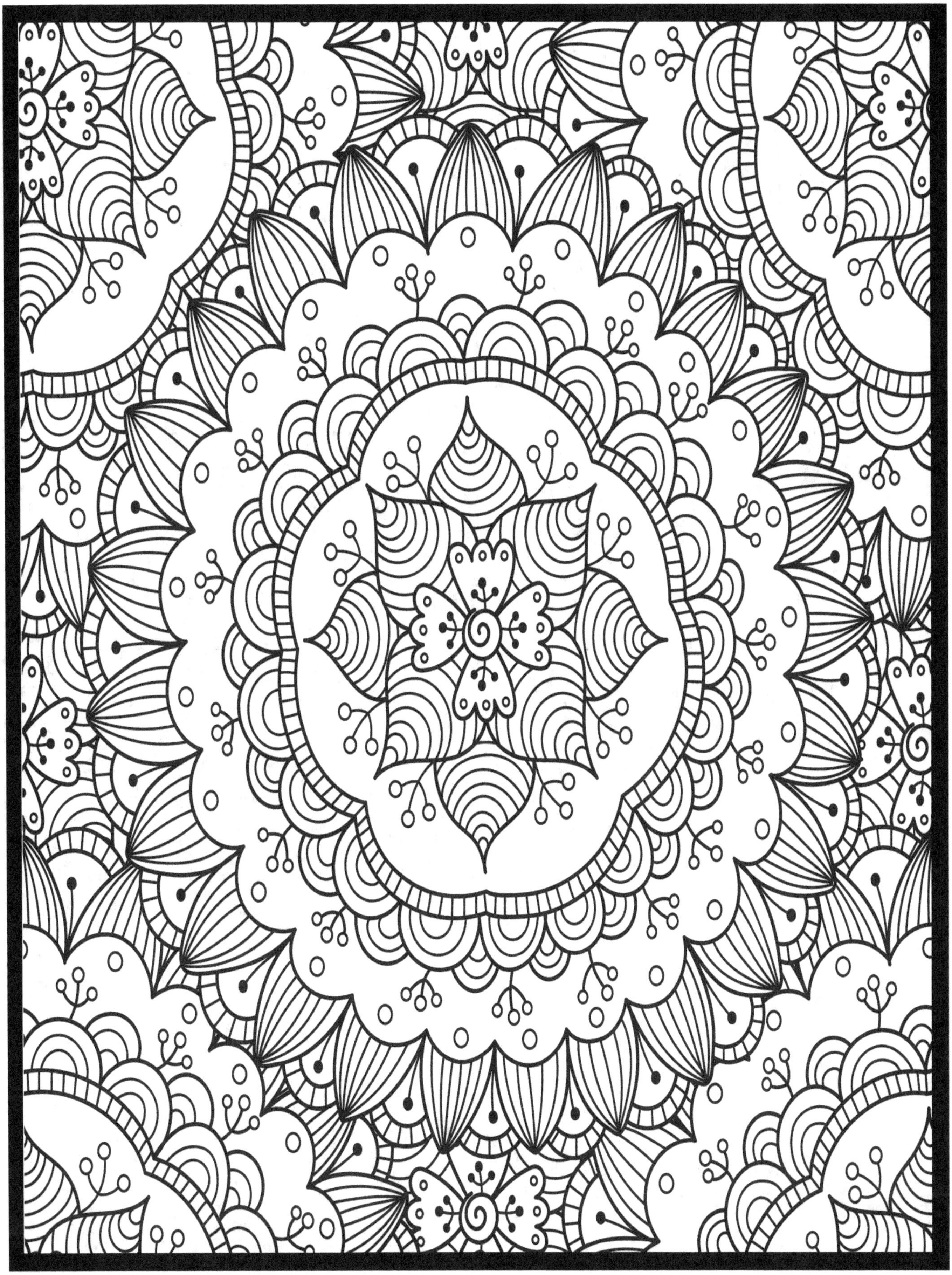

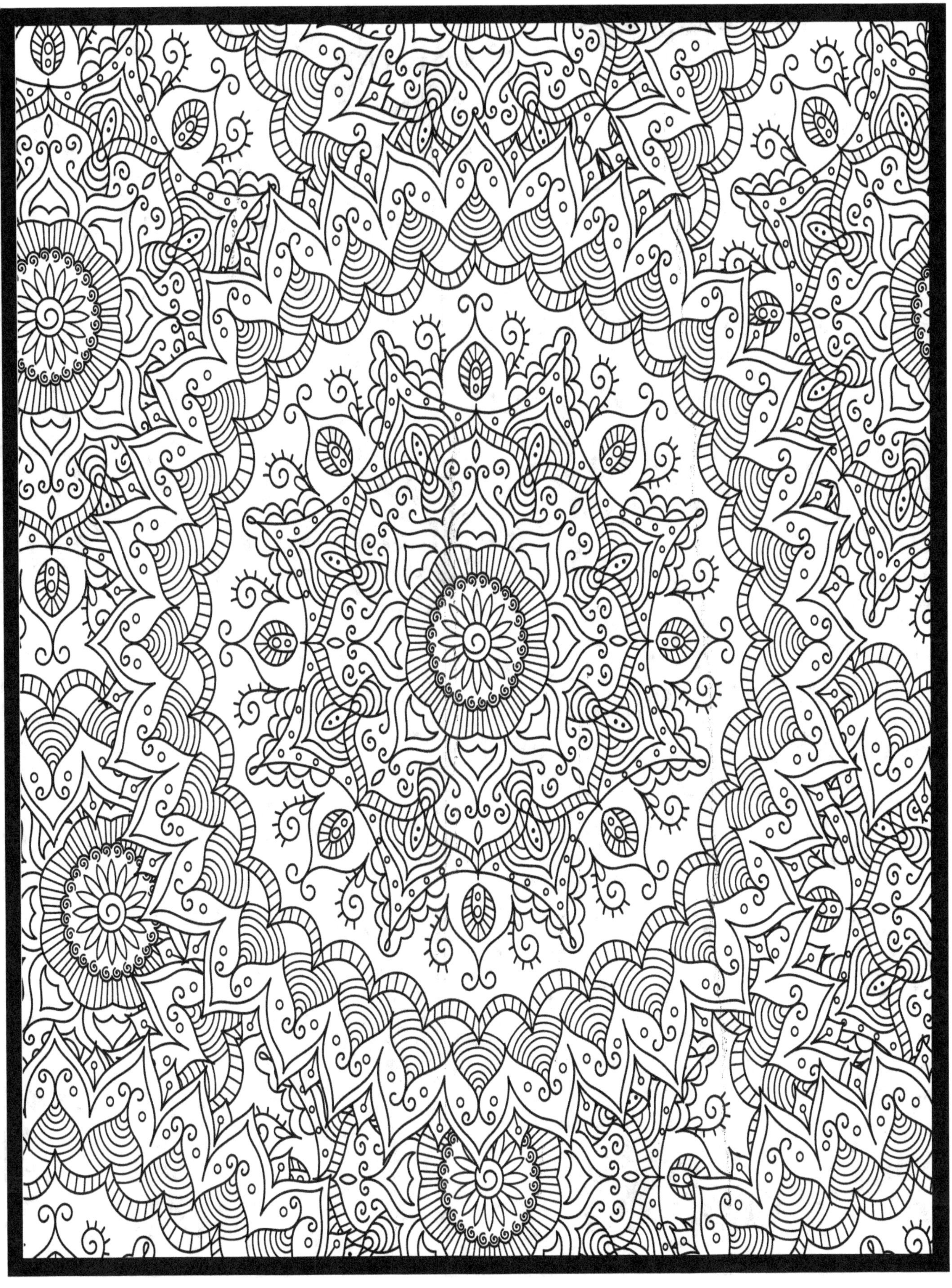

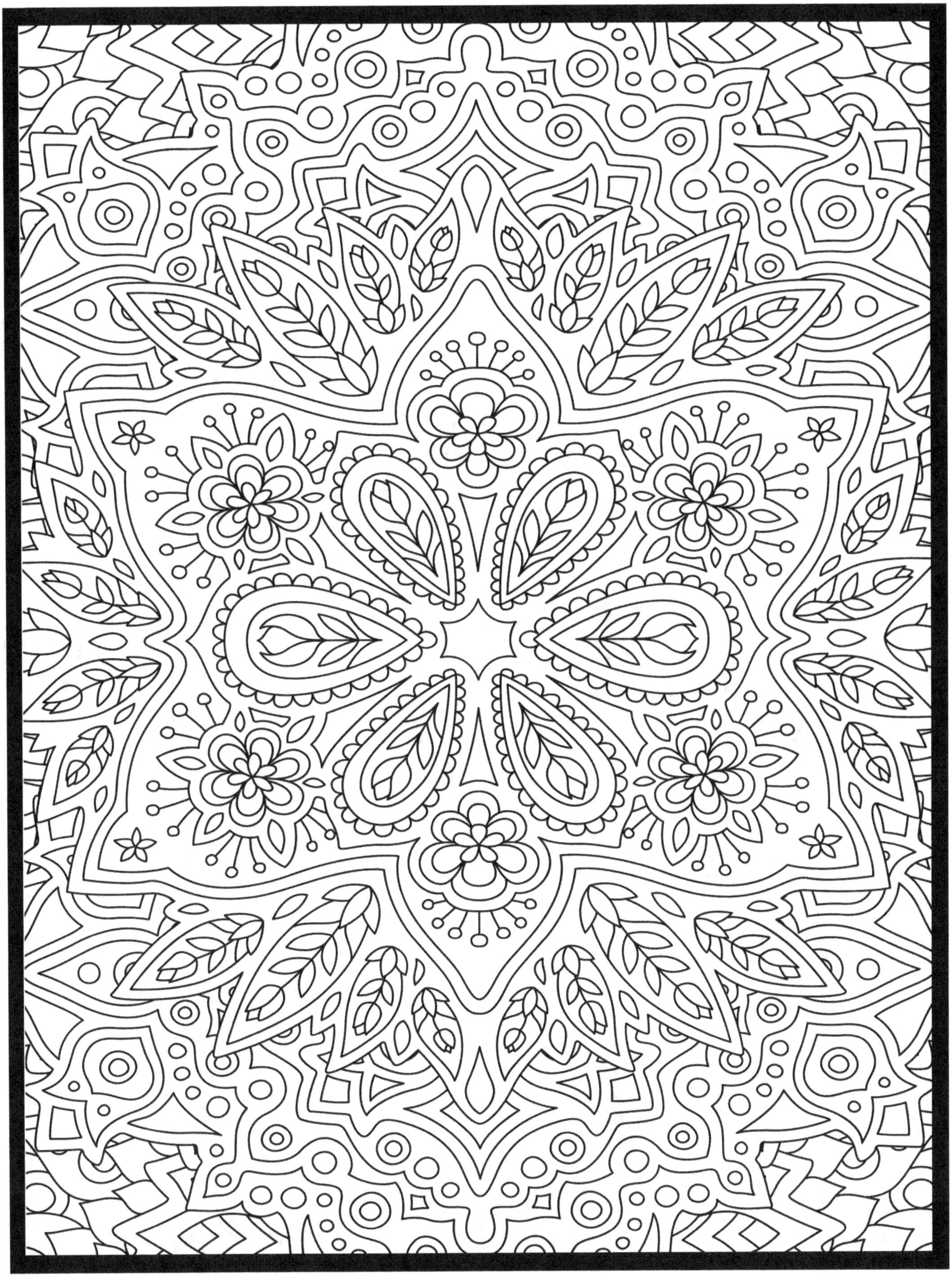

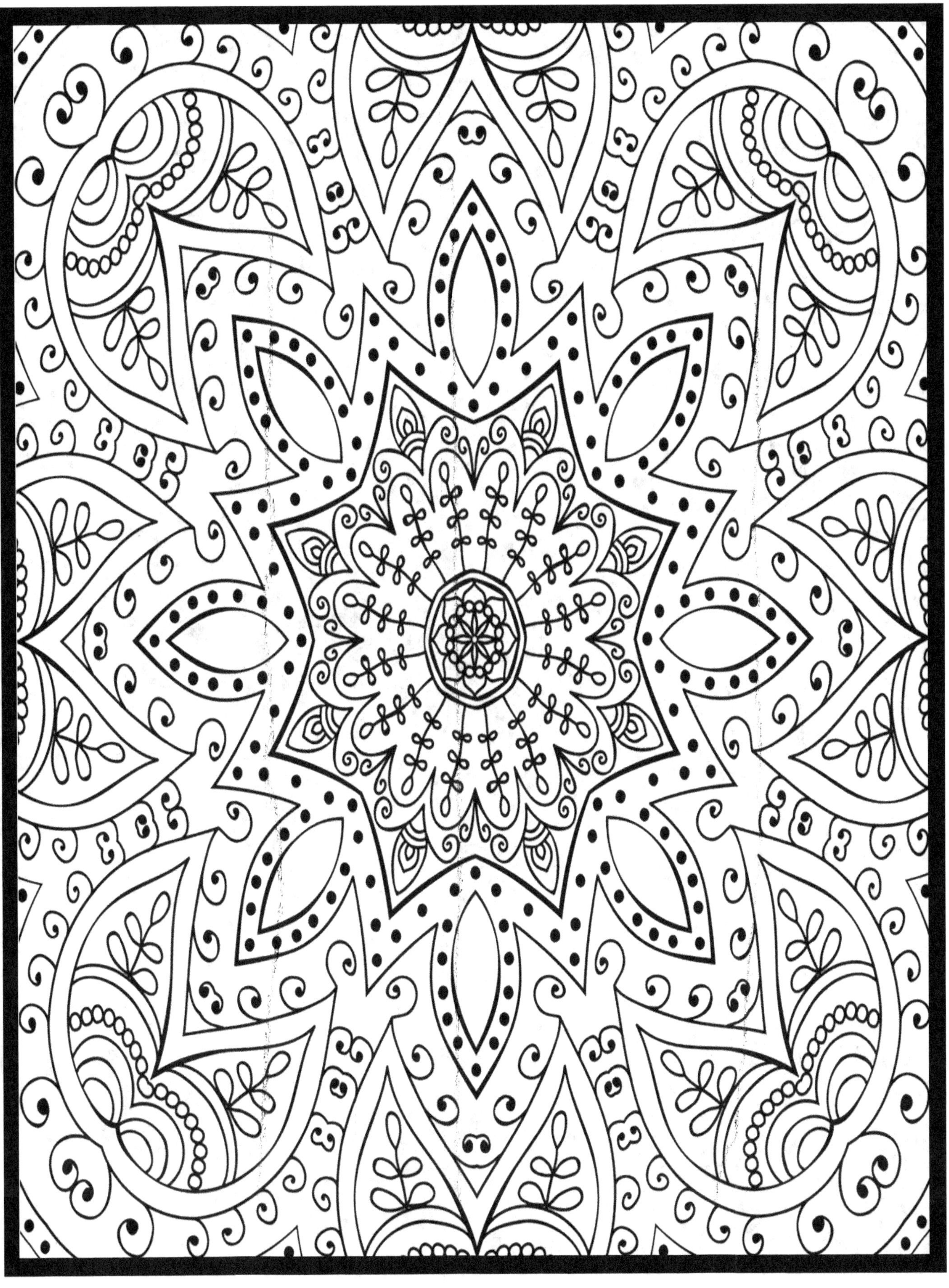

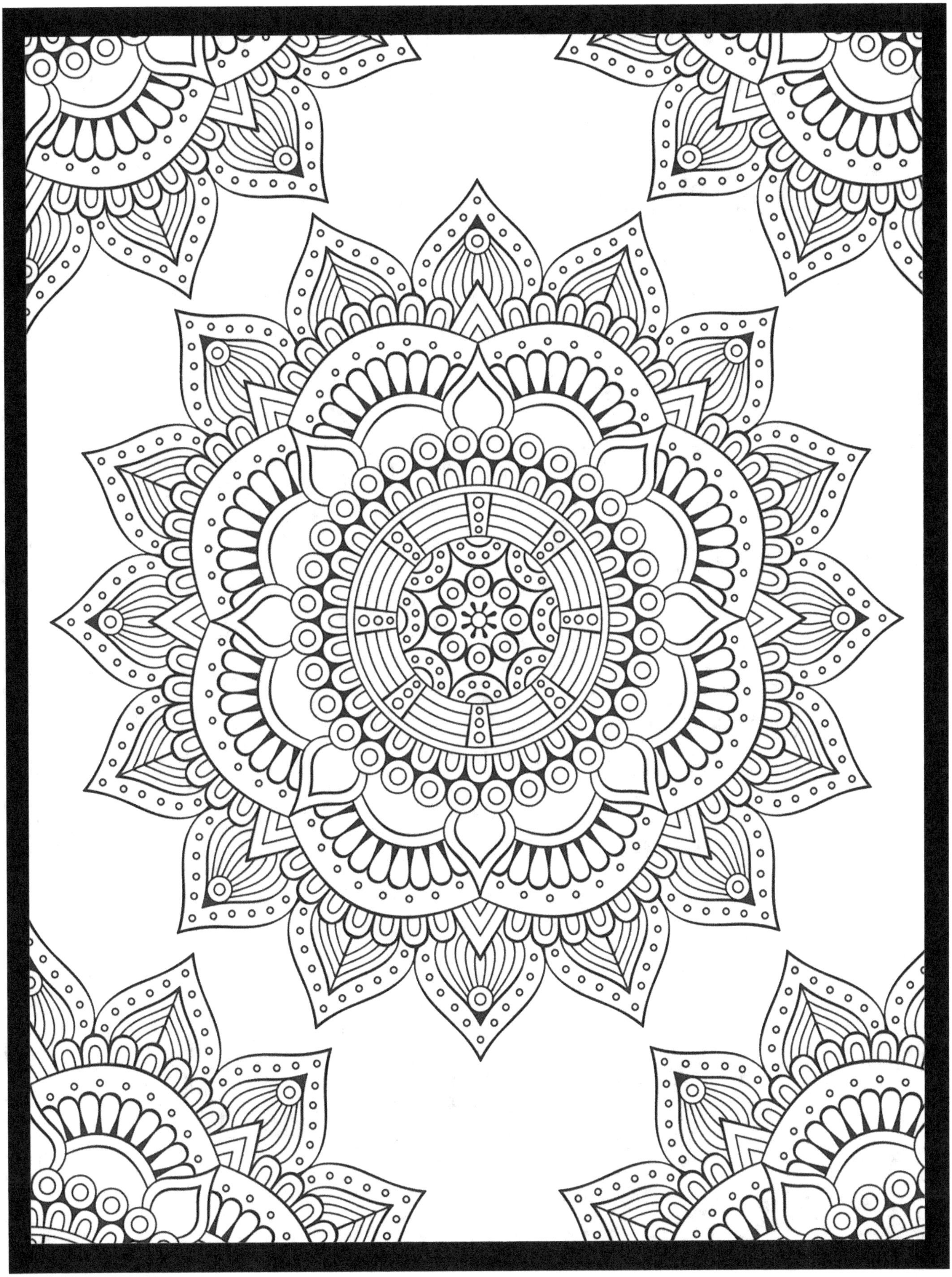

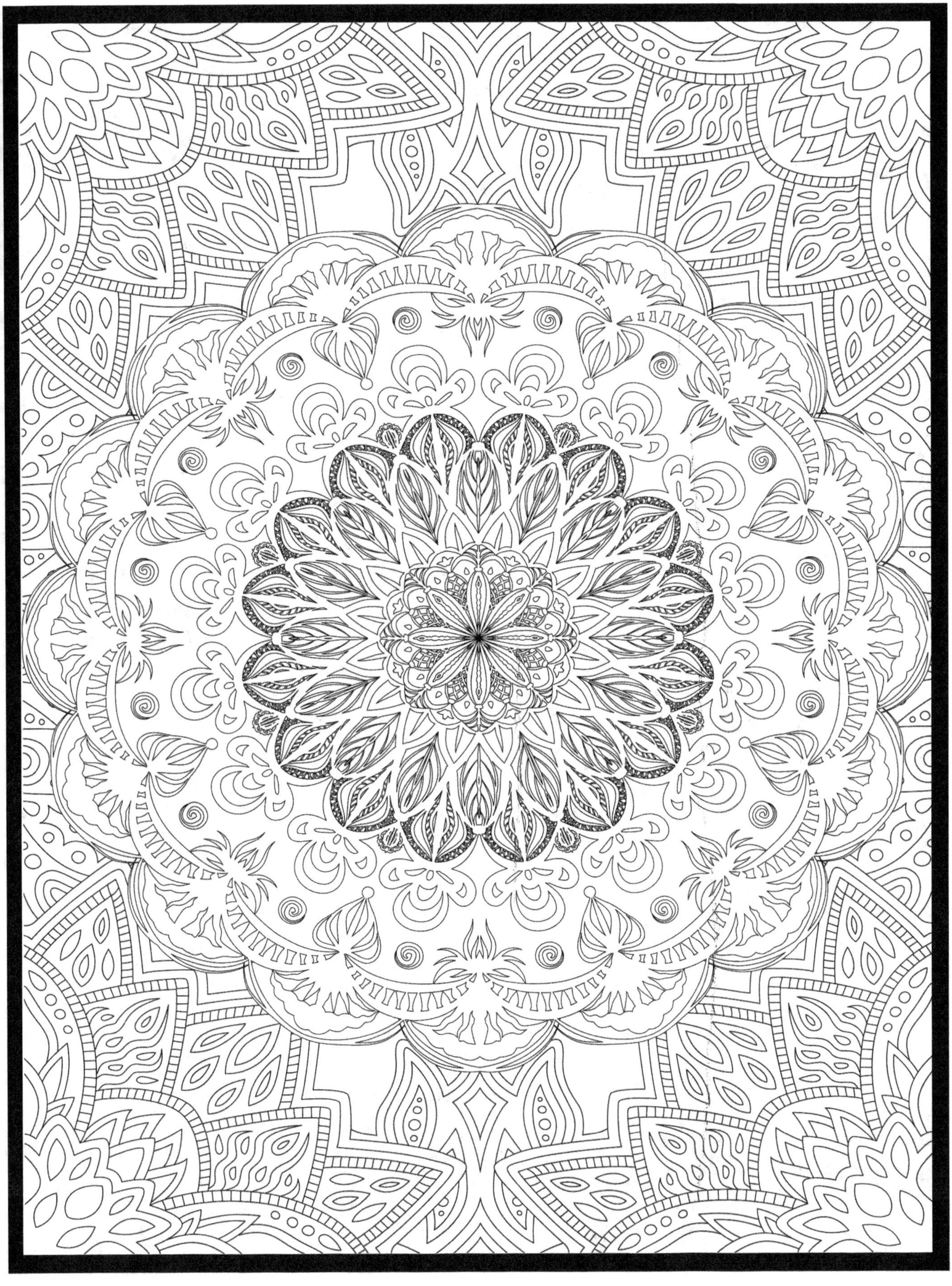

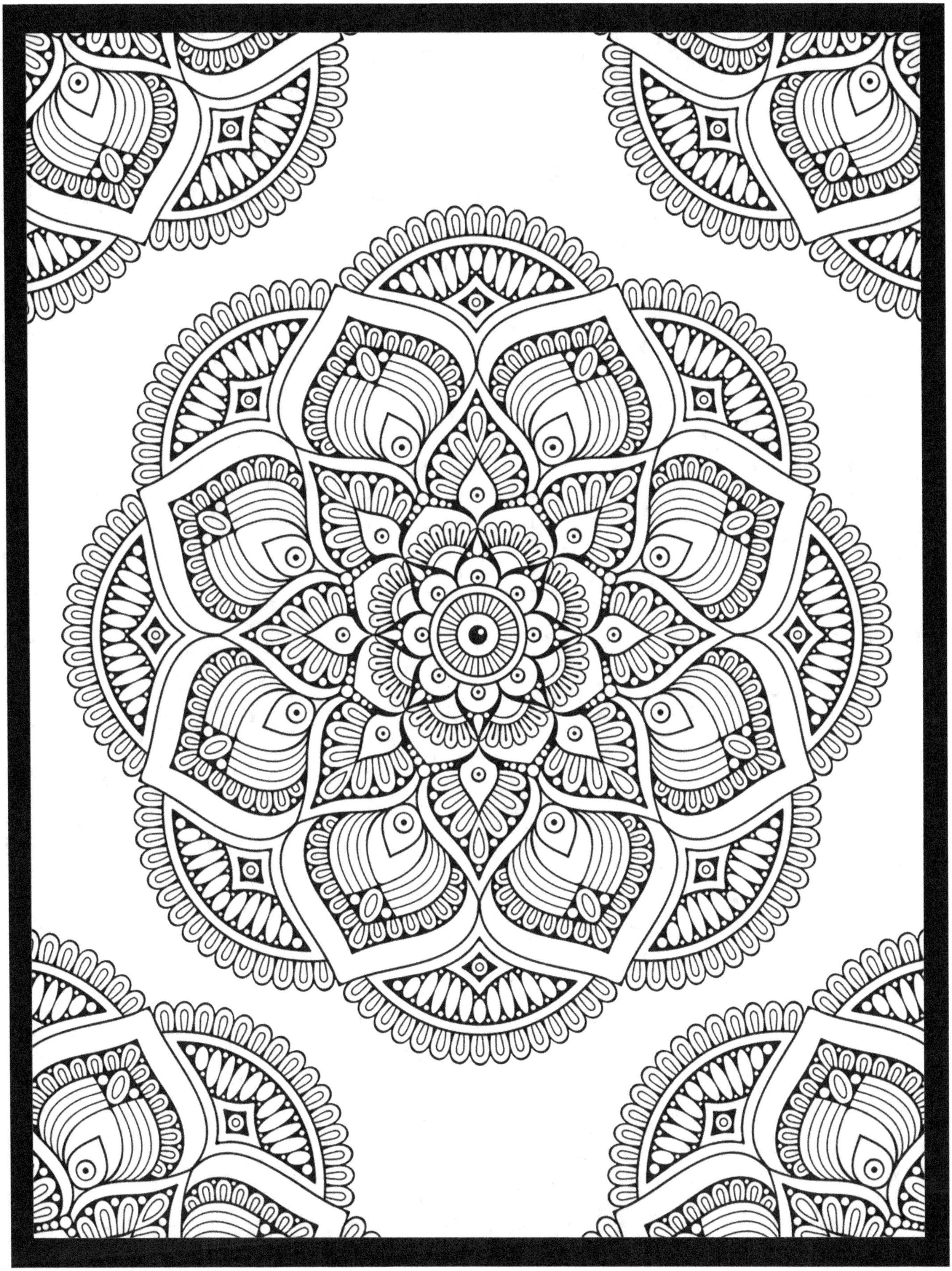

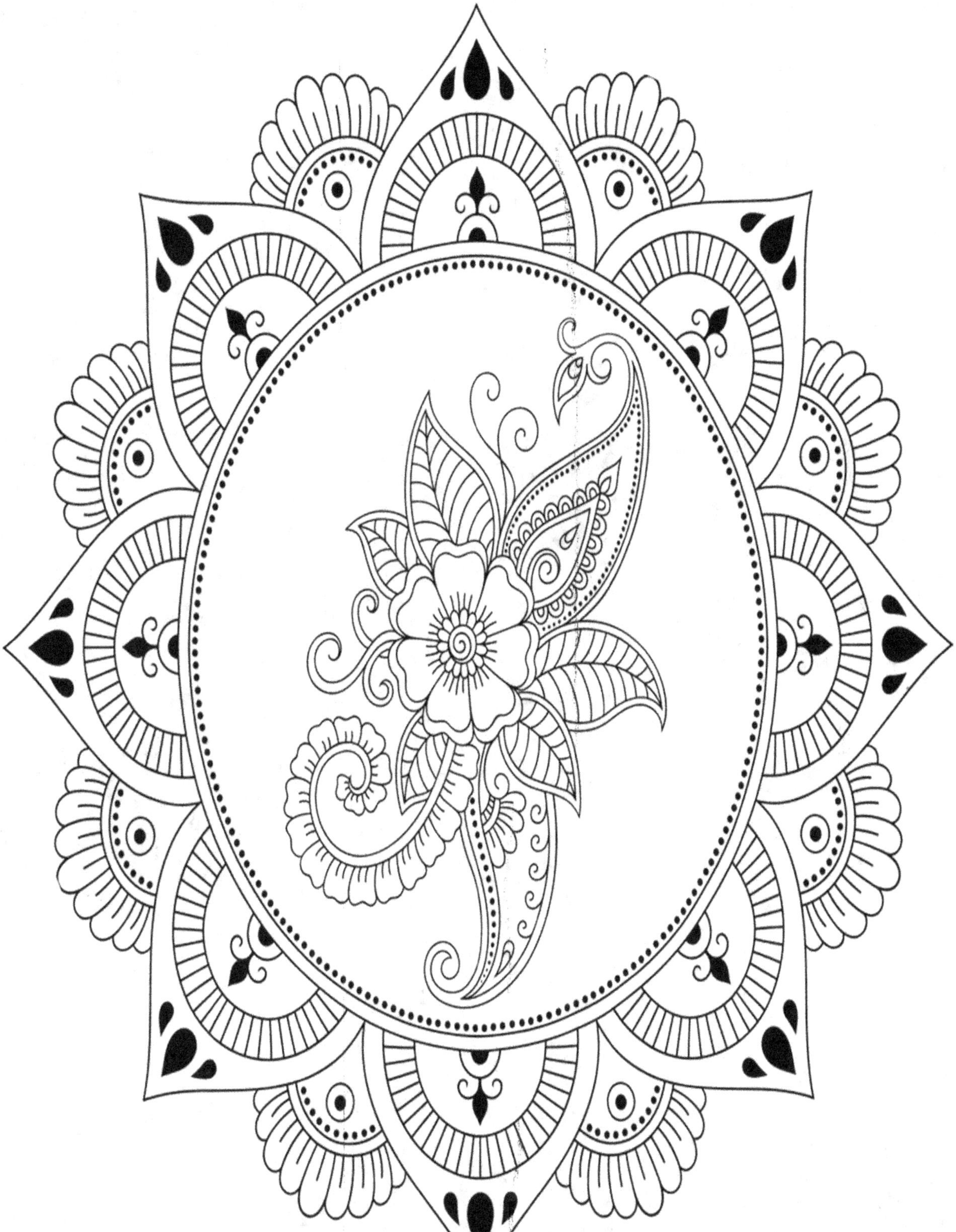

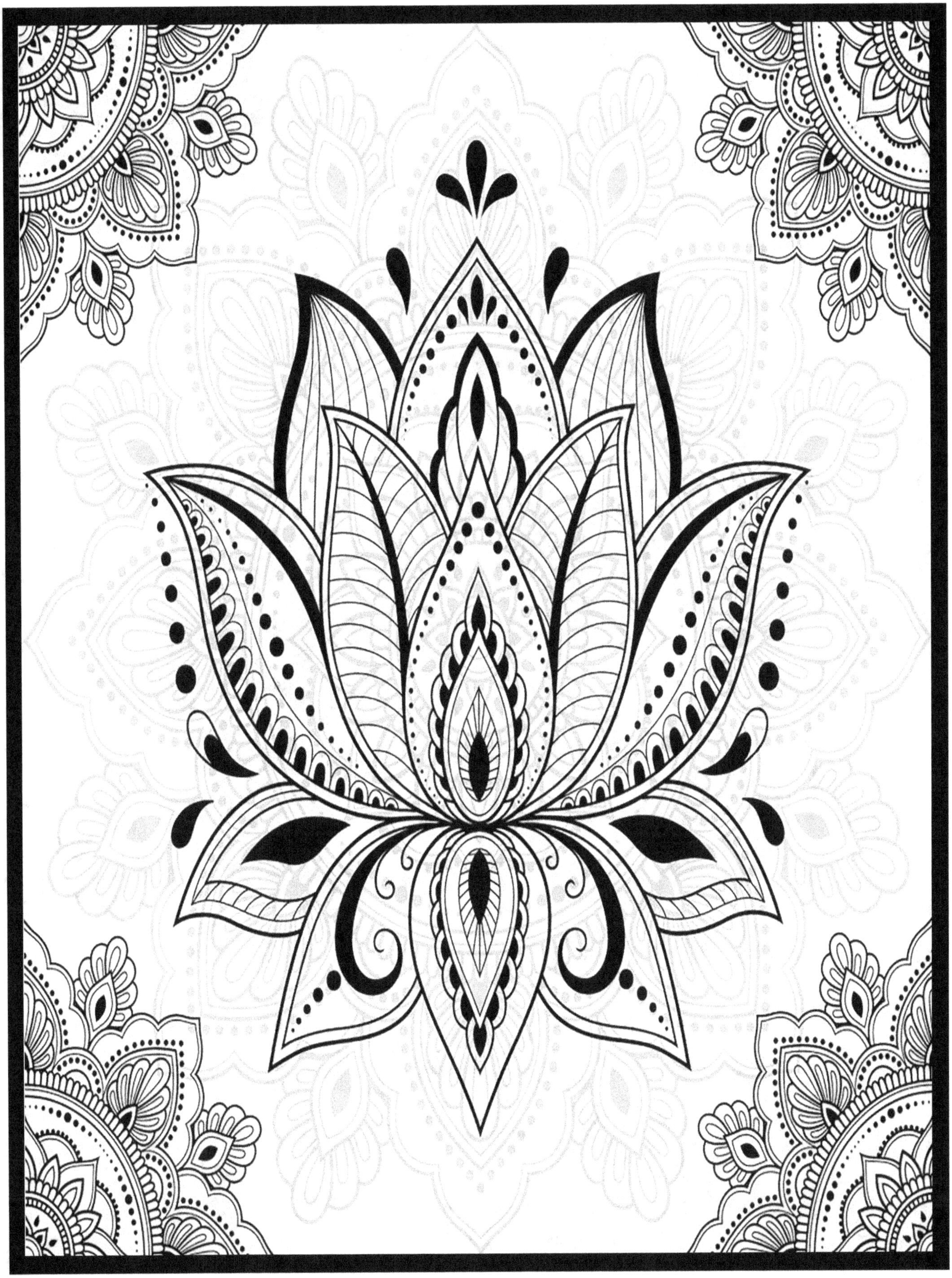

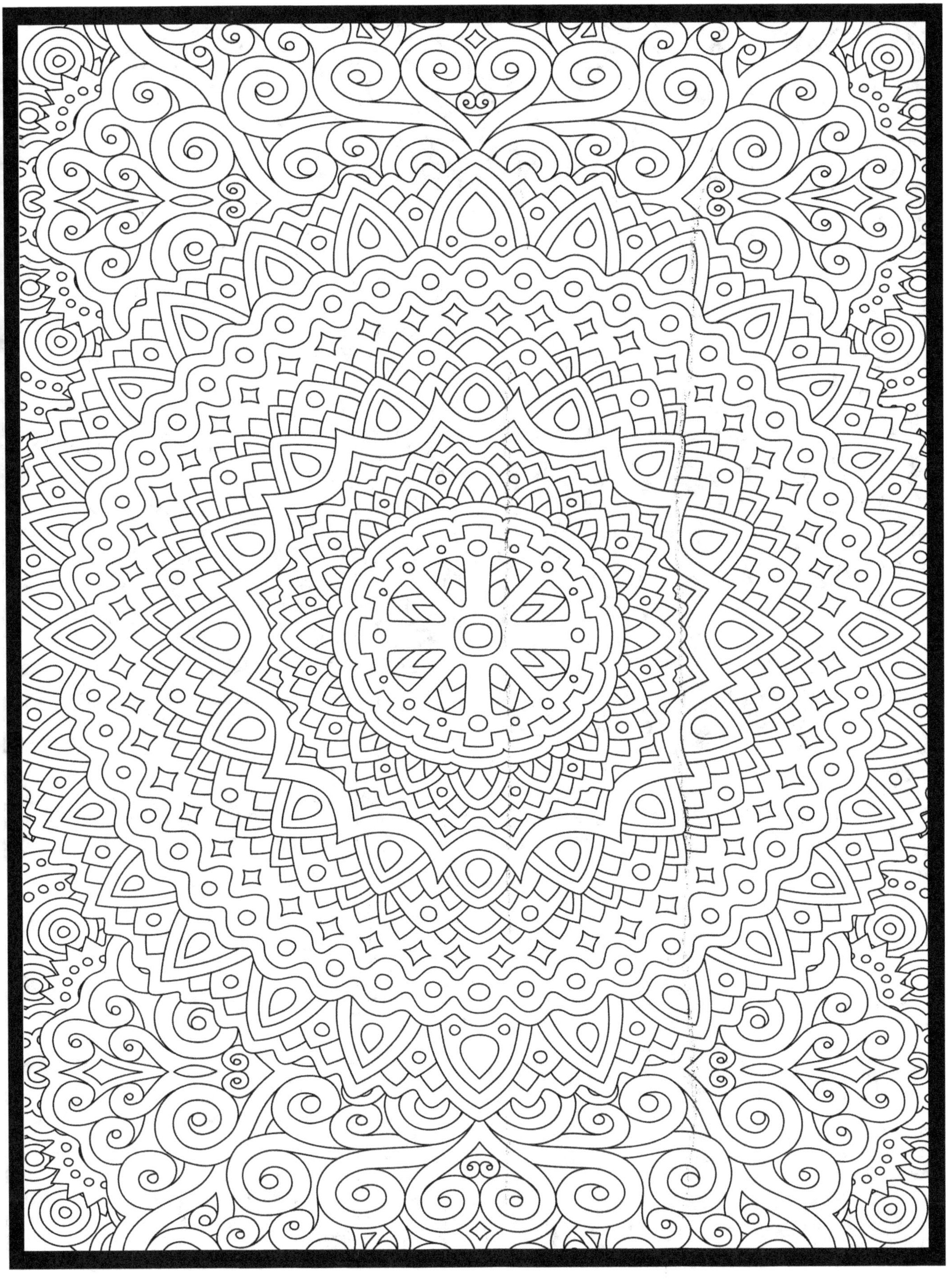

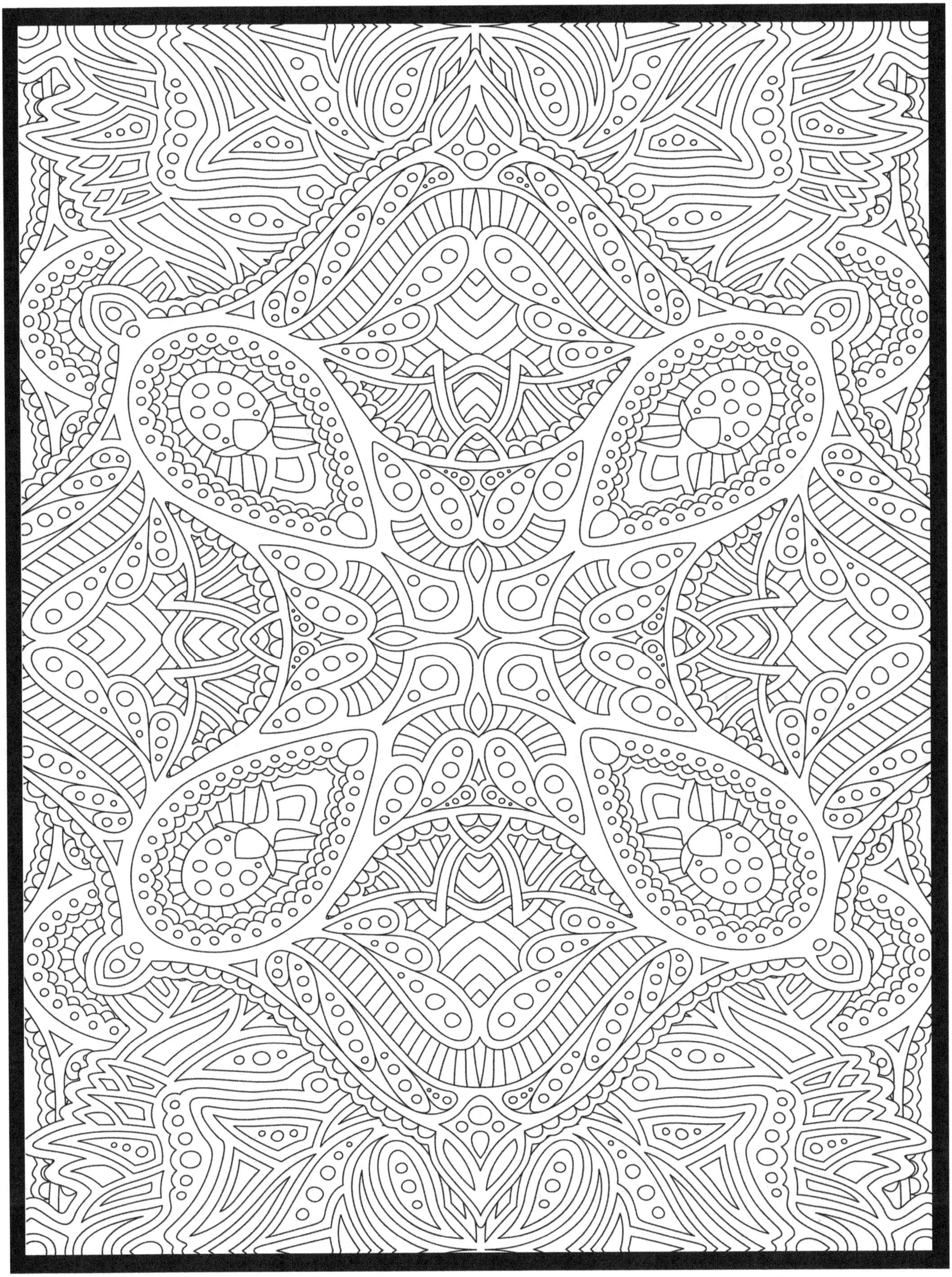

[redacted]

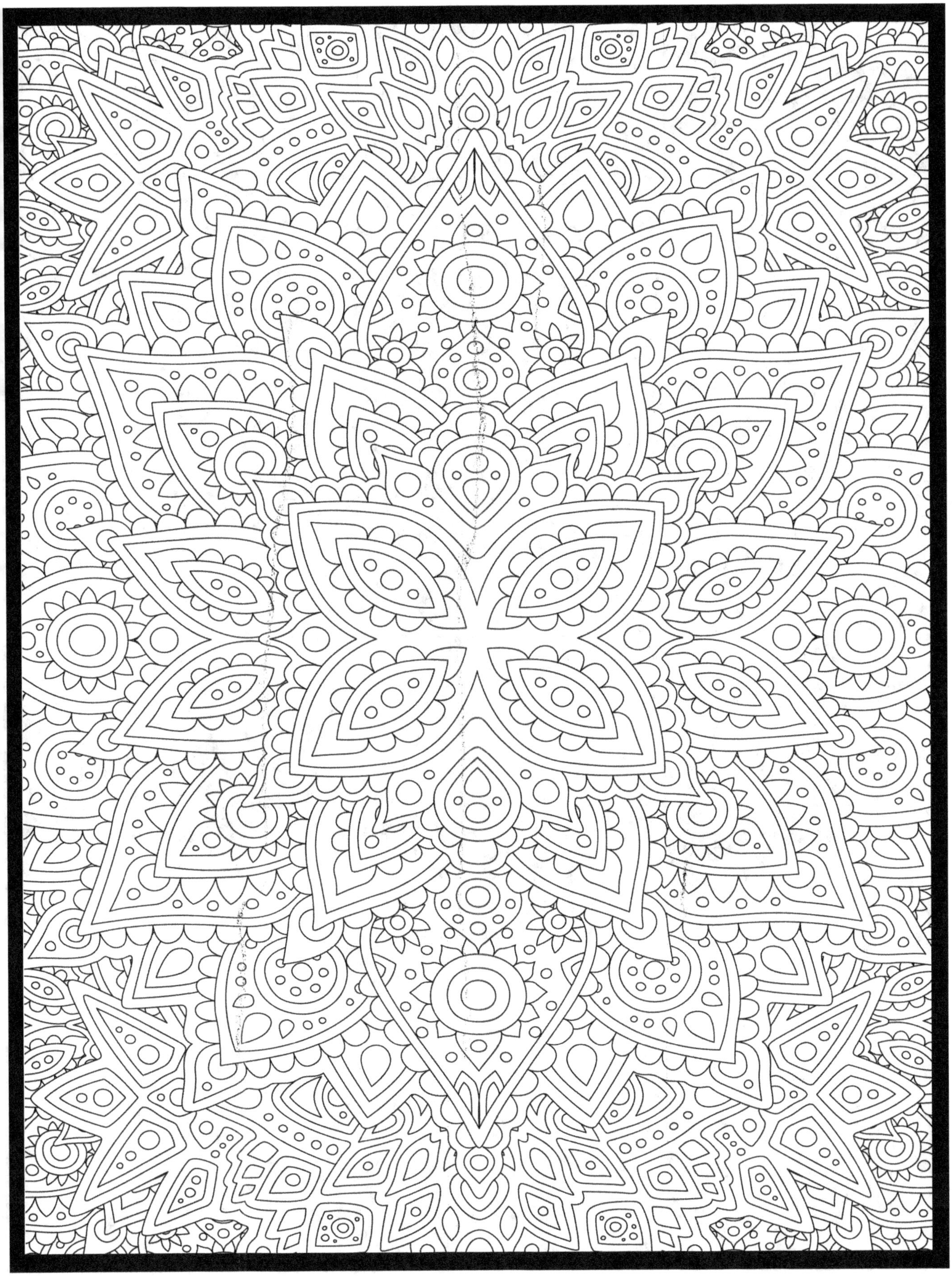

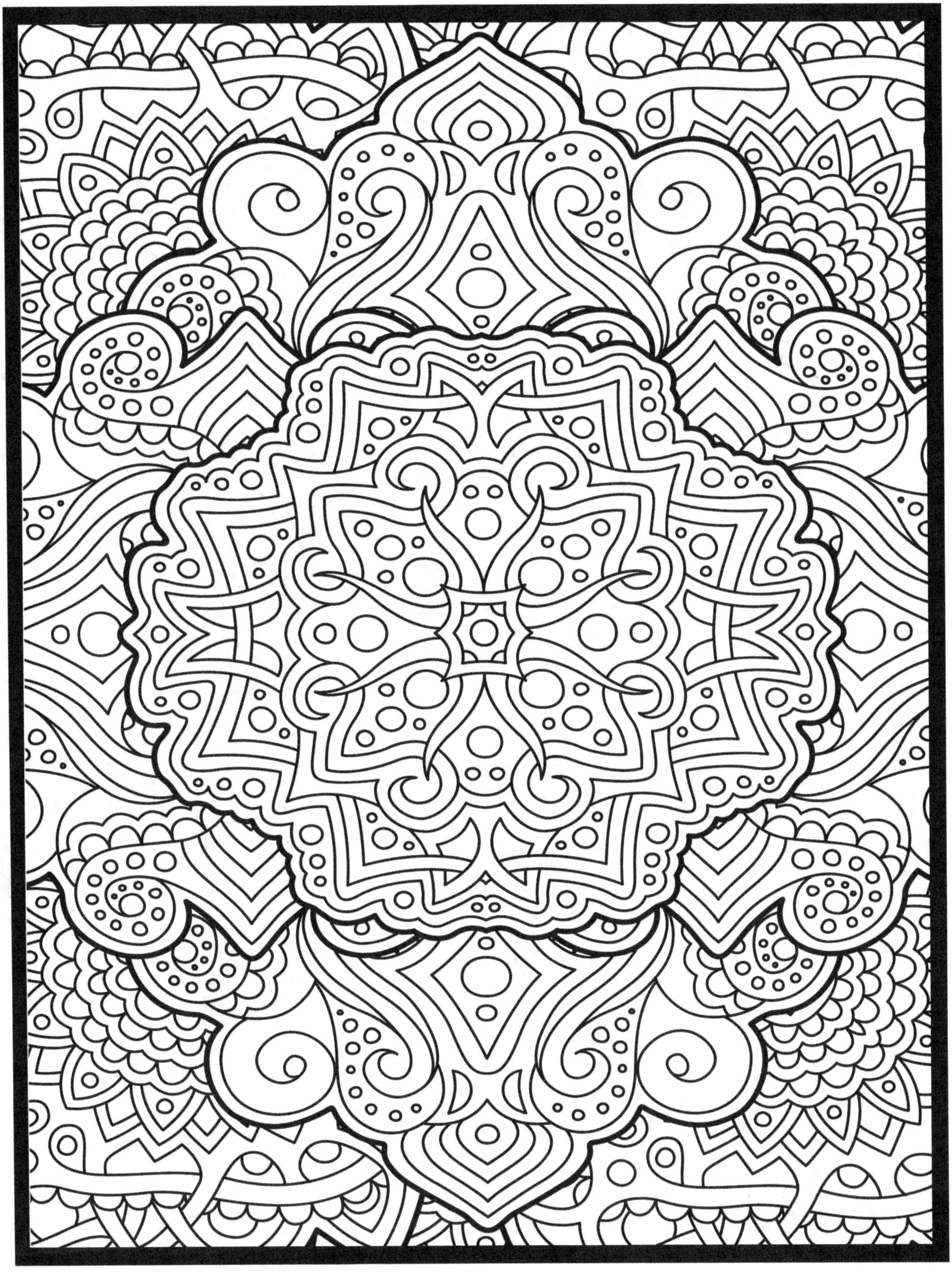

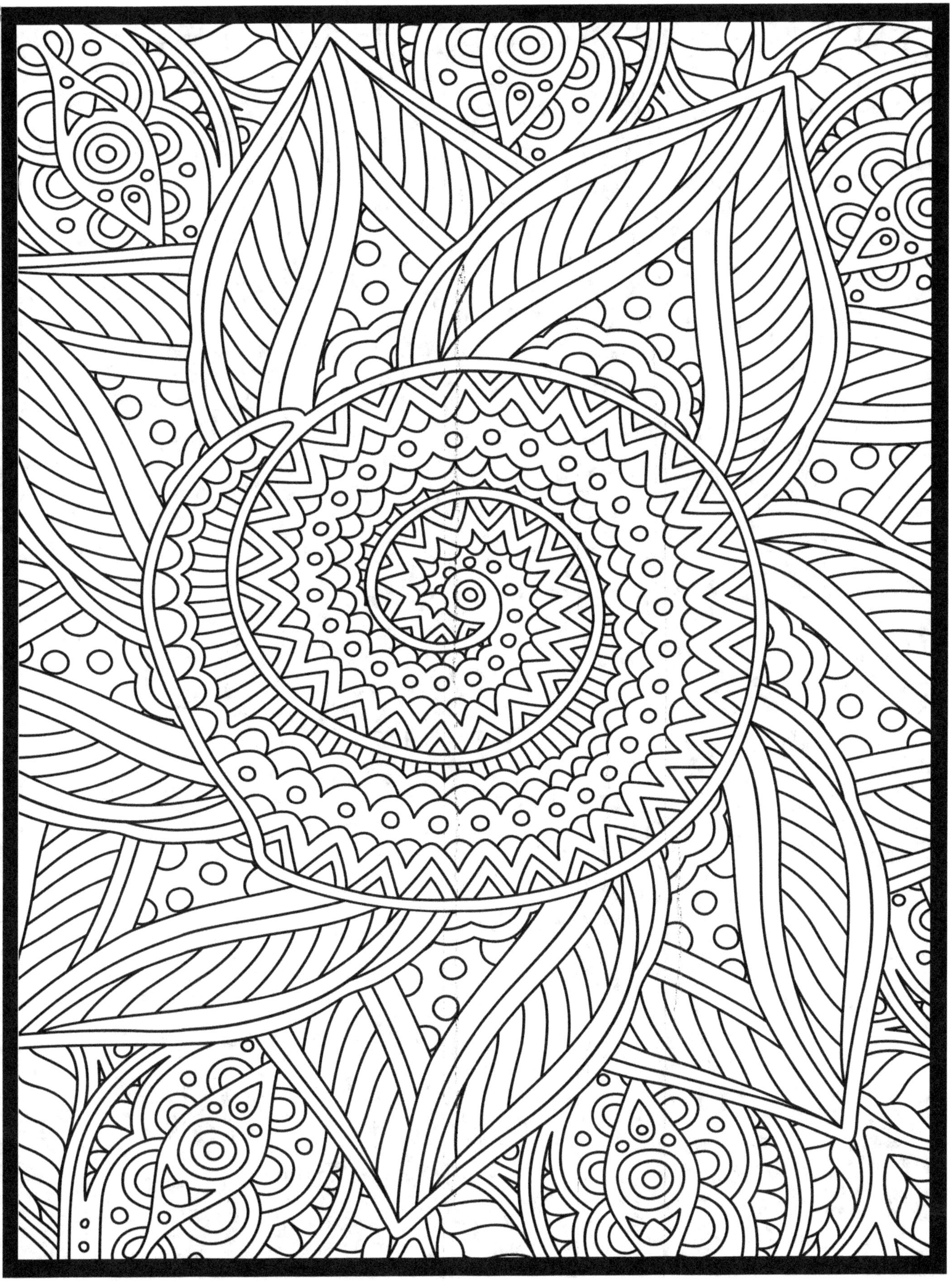

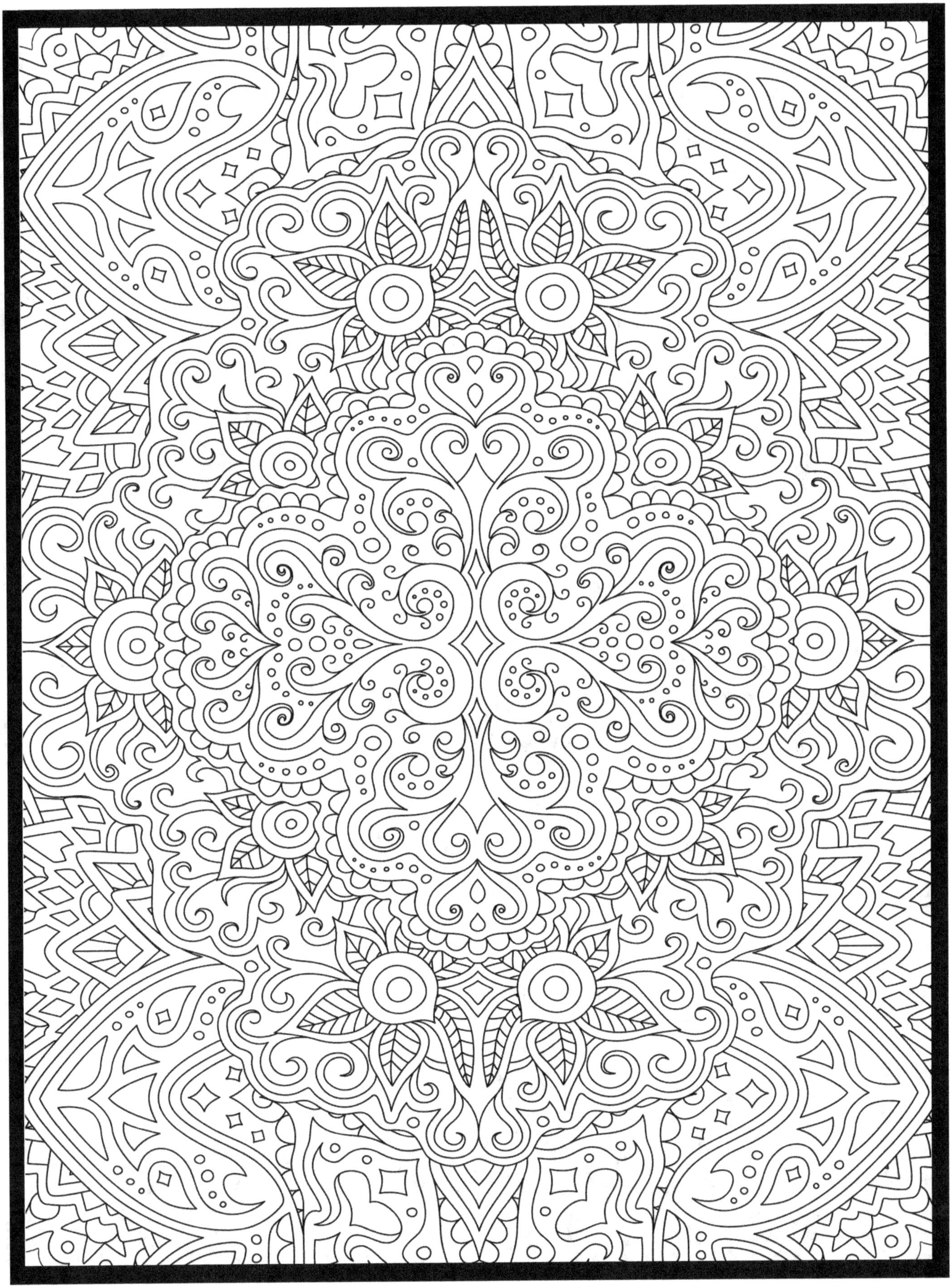

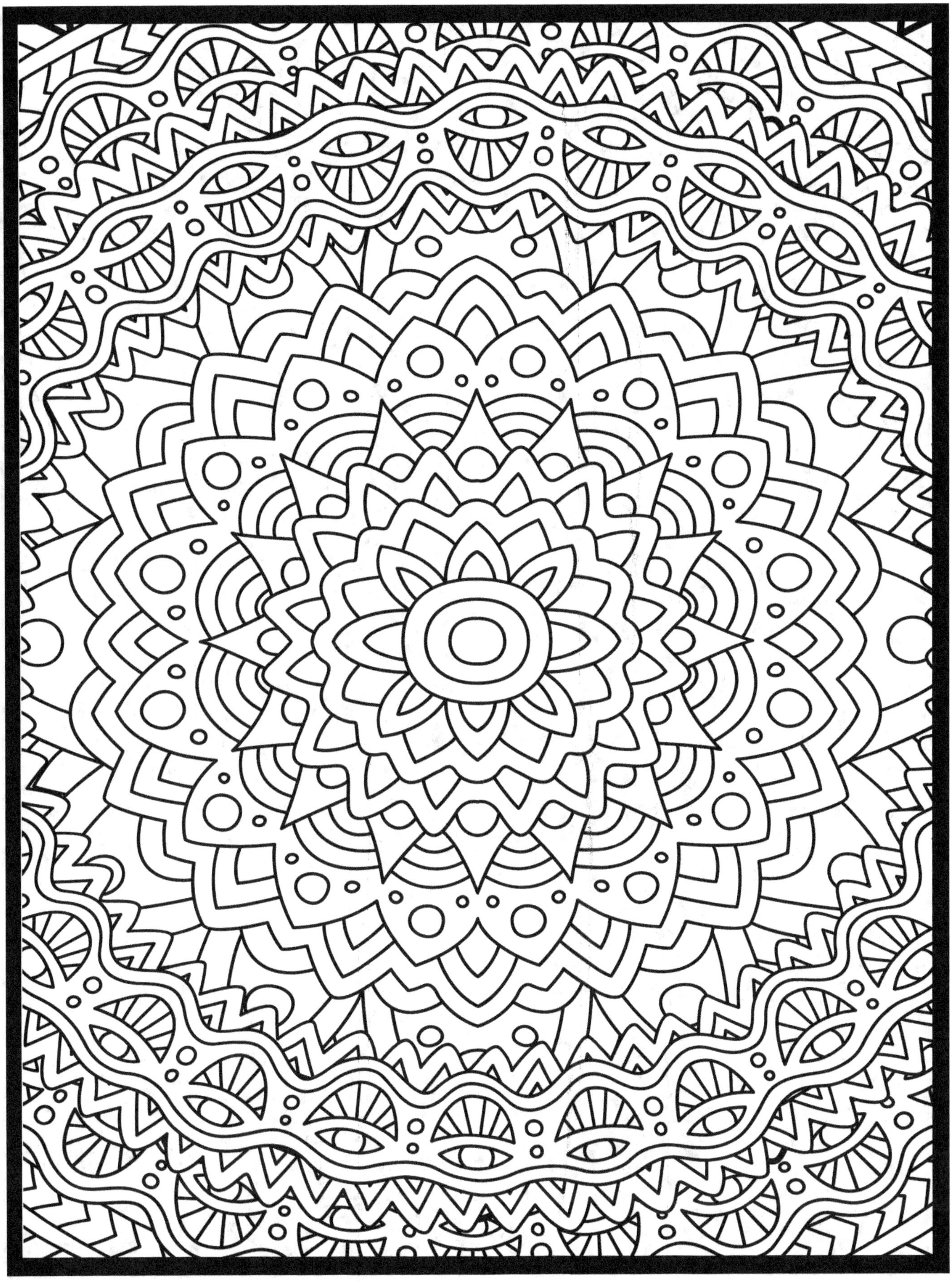

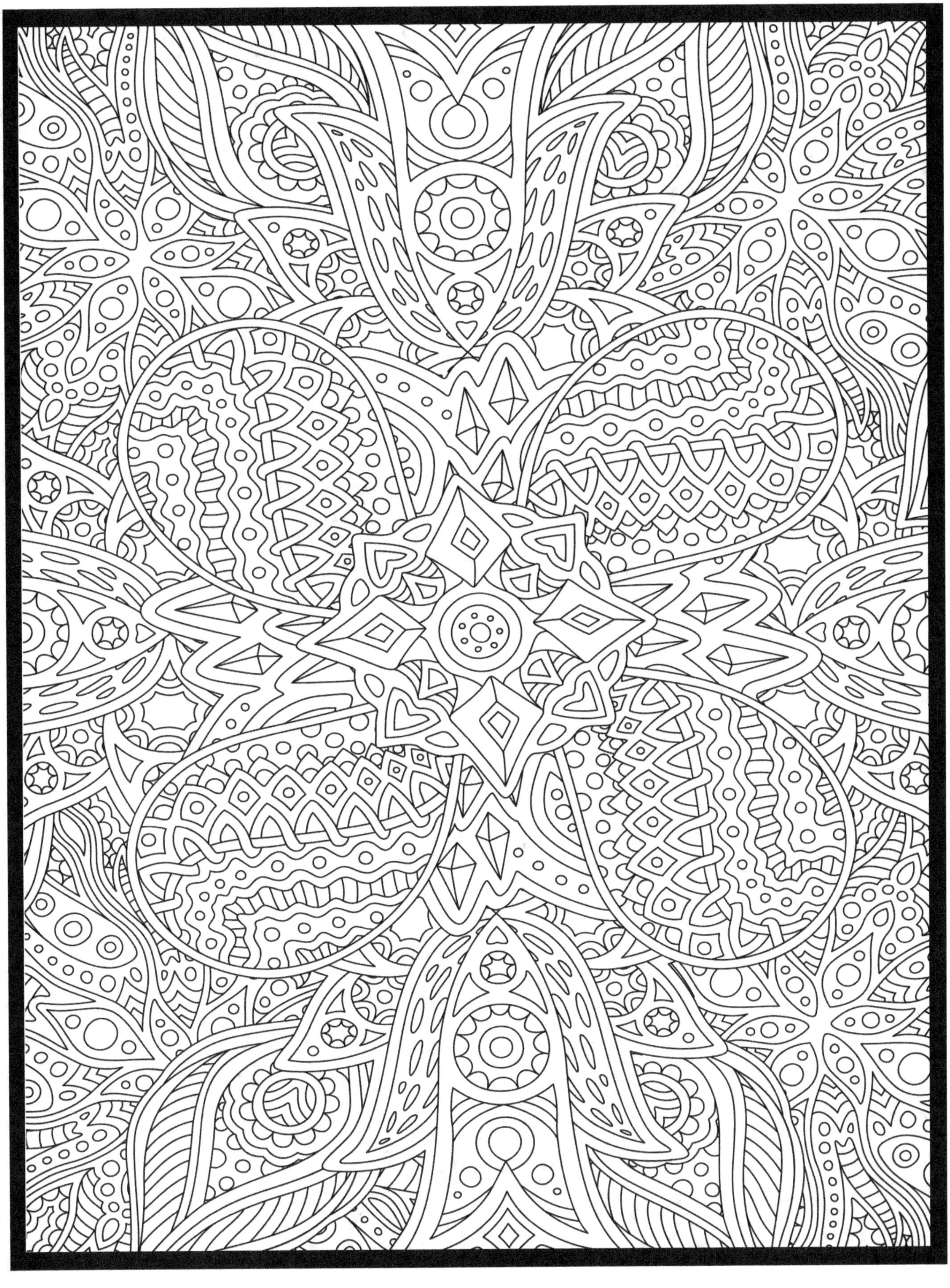

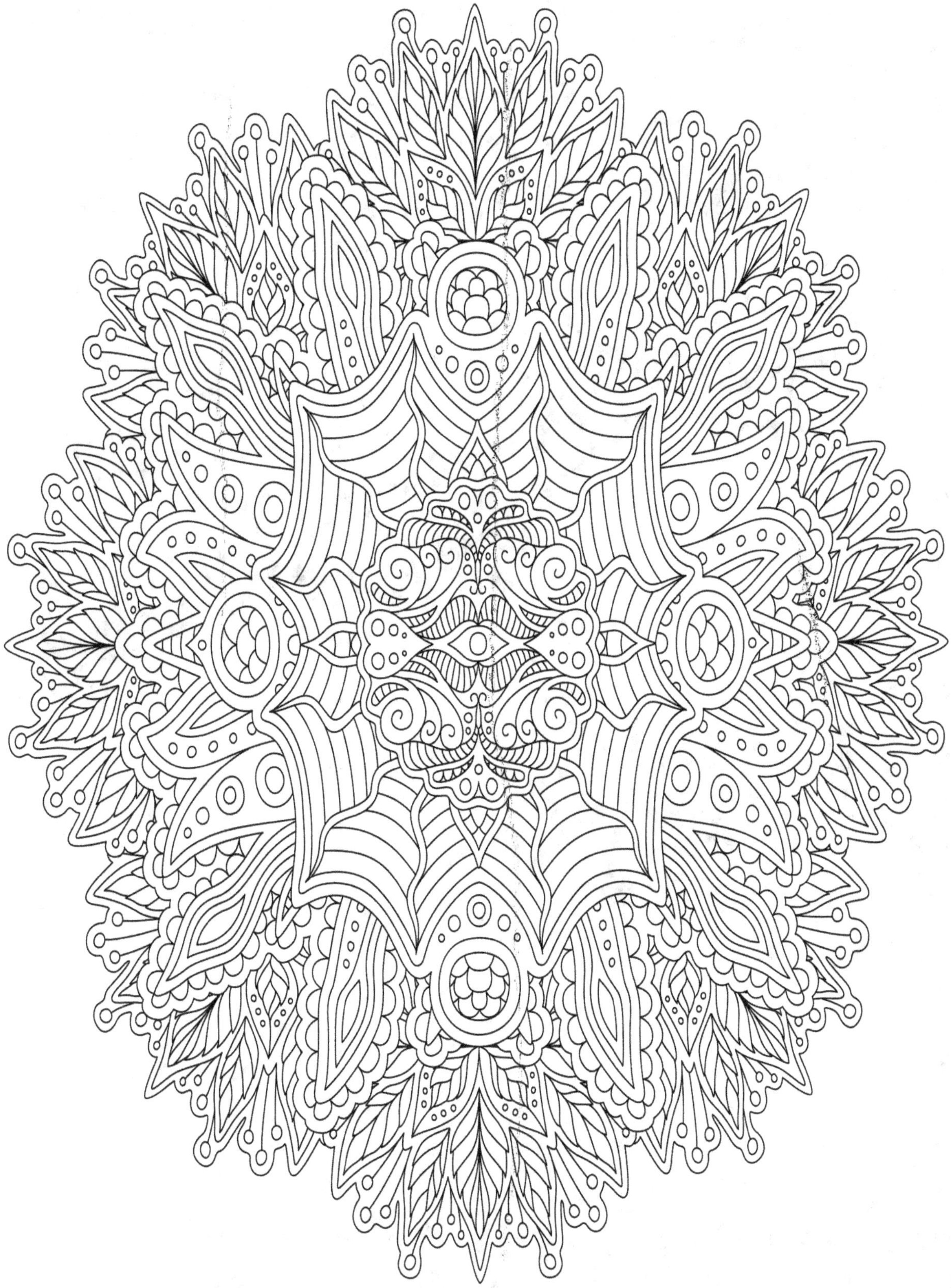

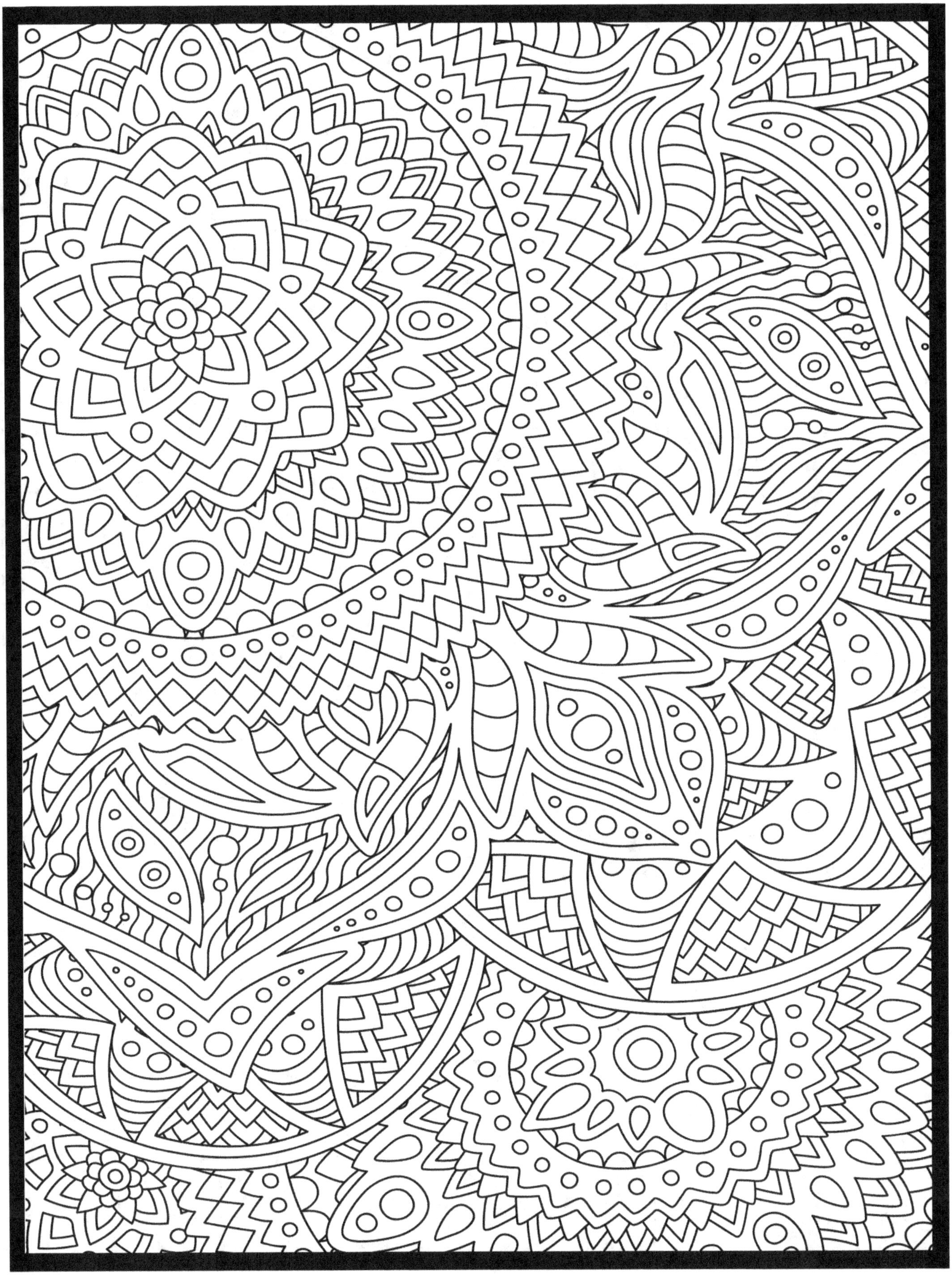

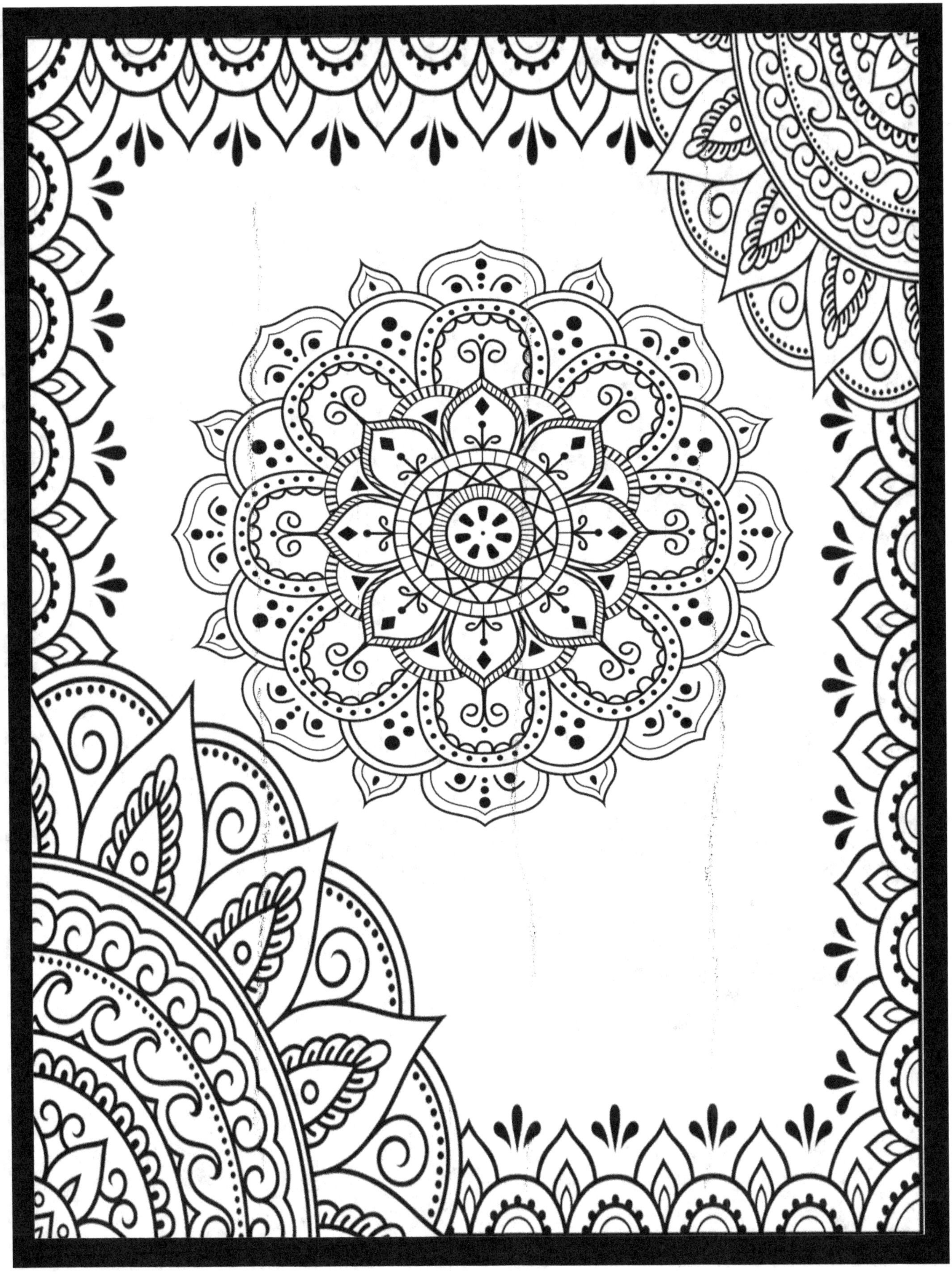

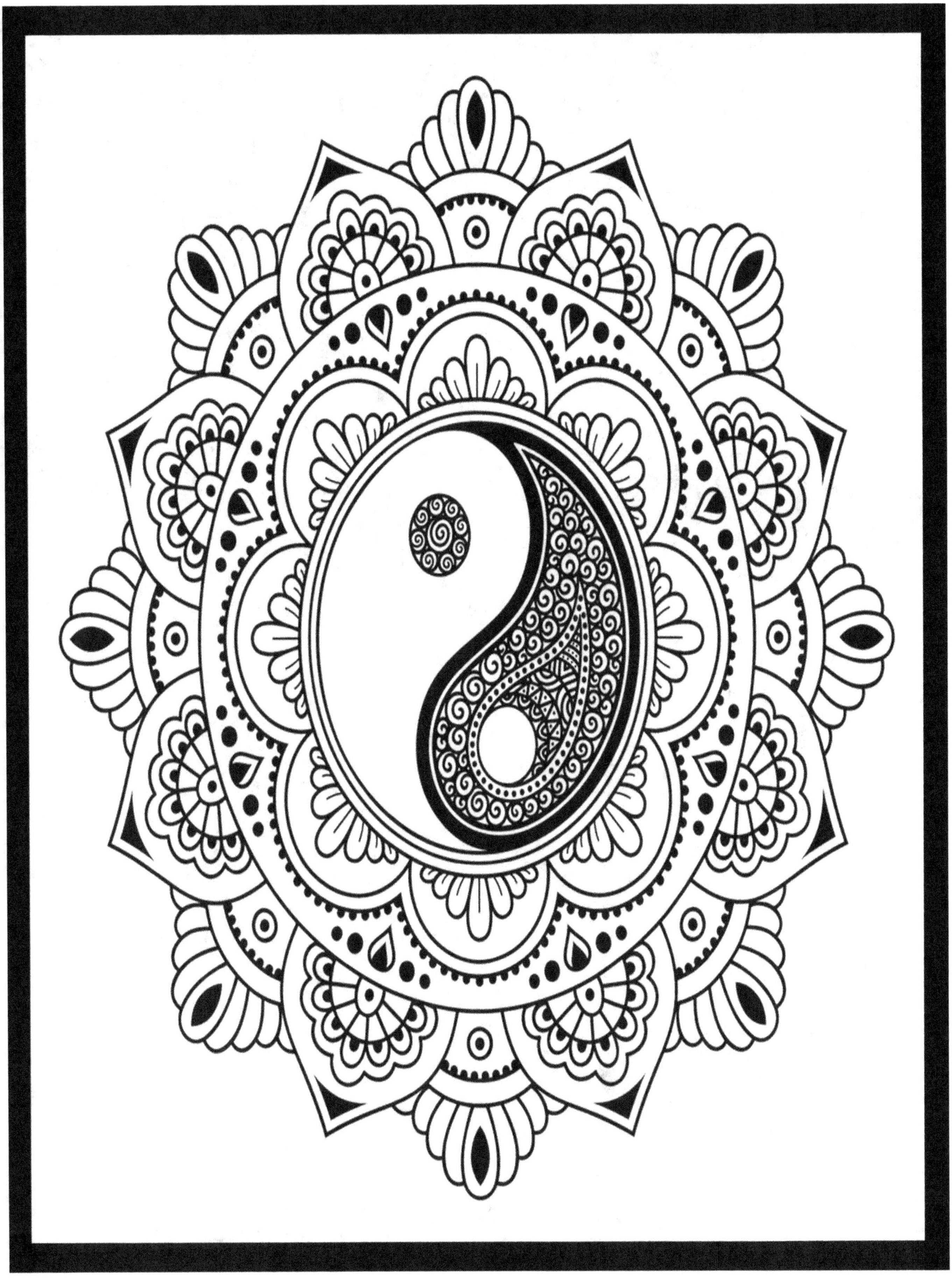

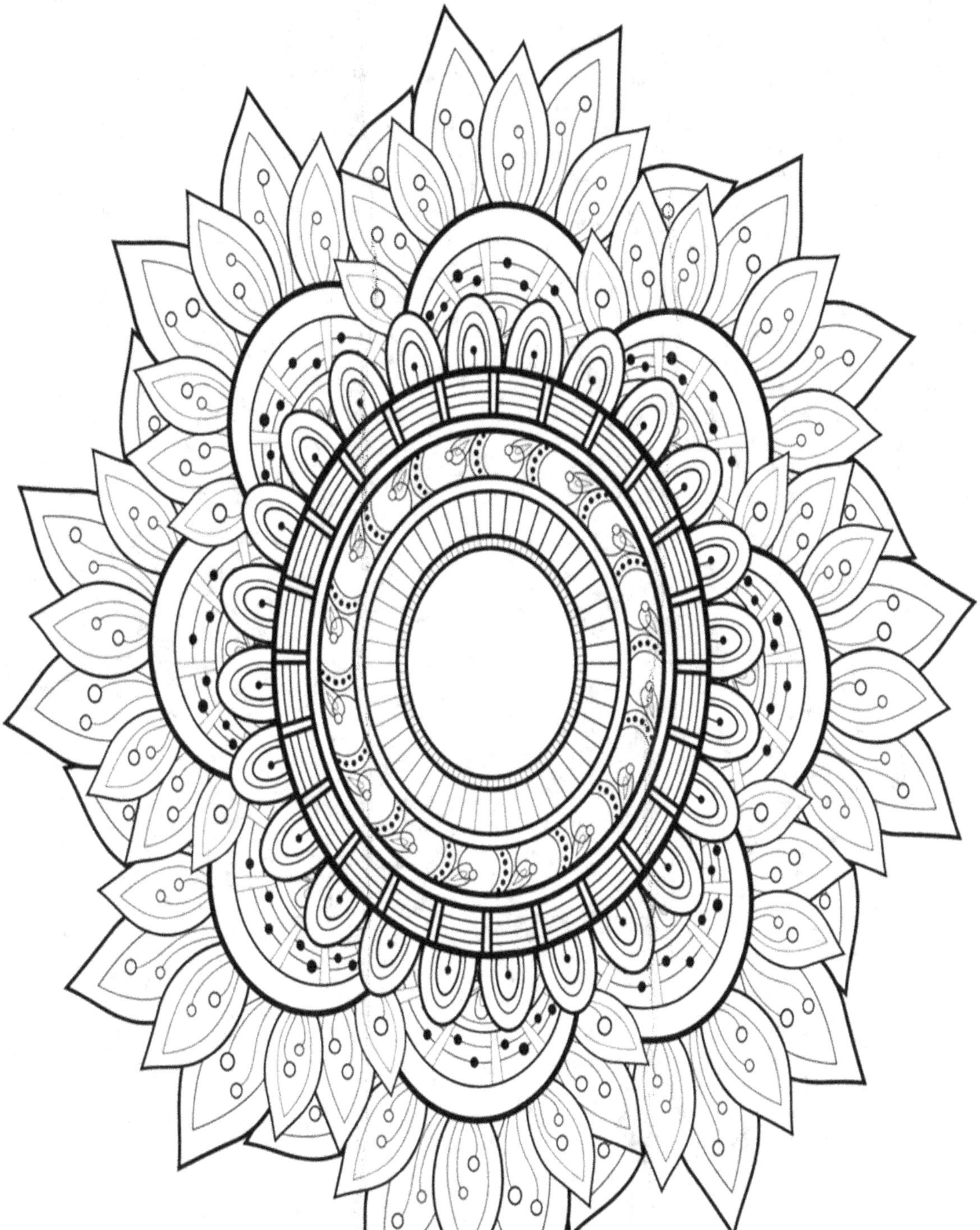

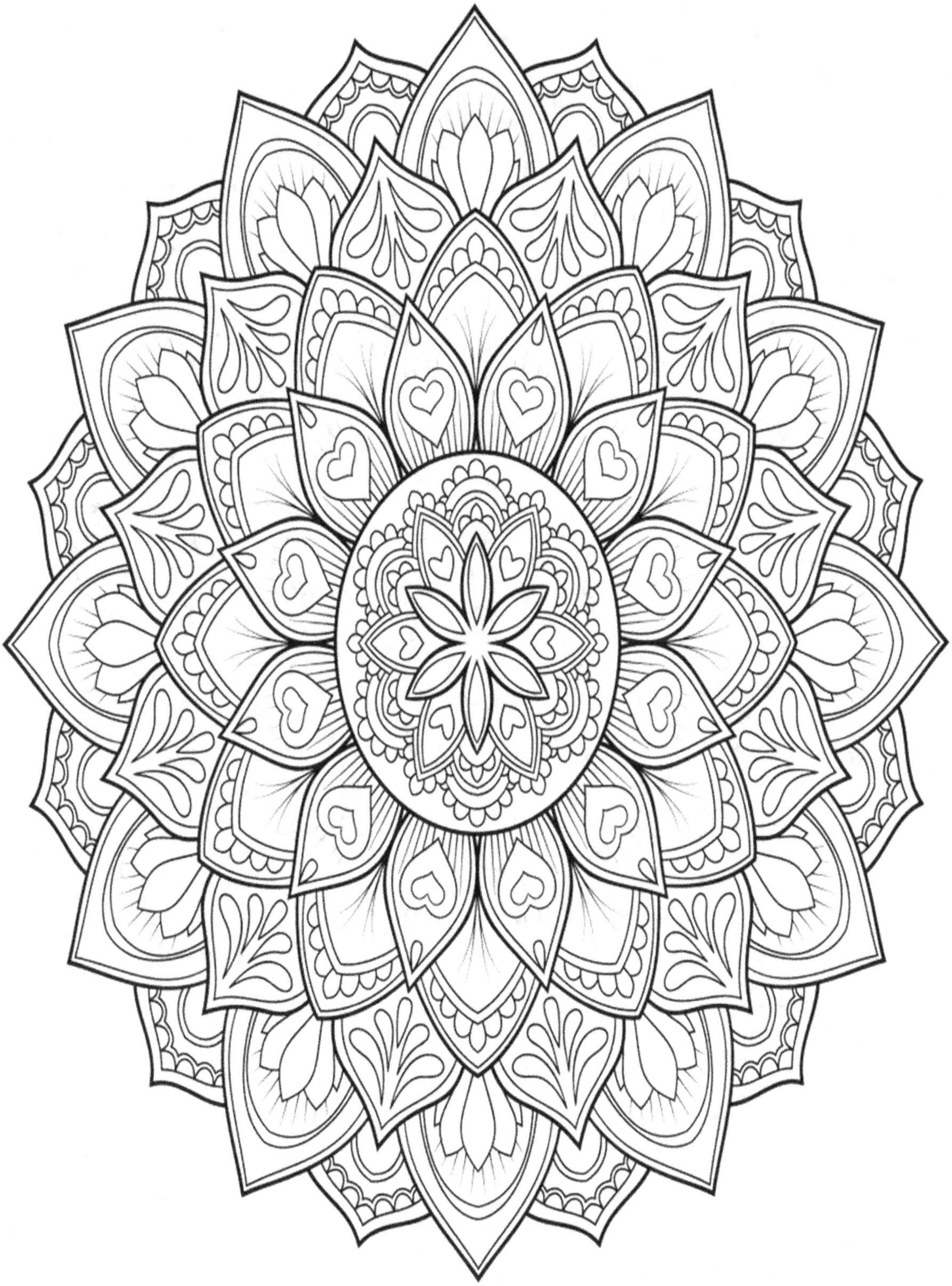

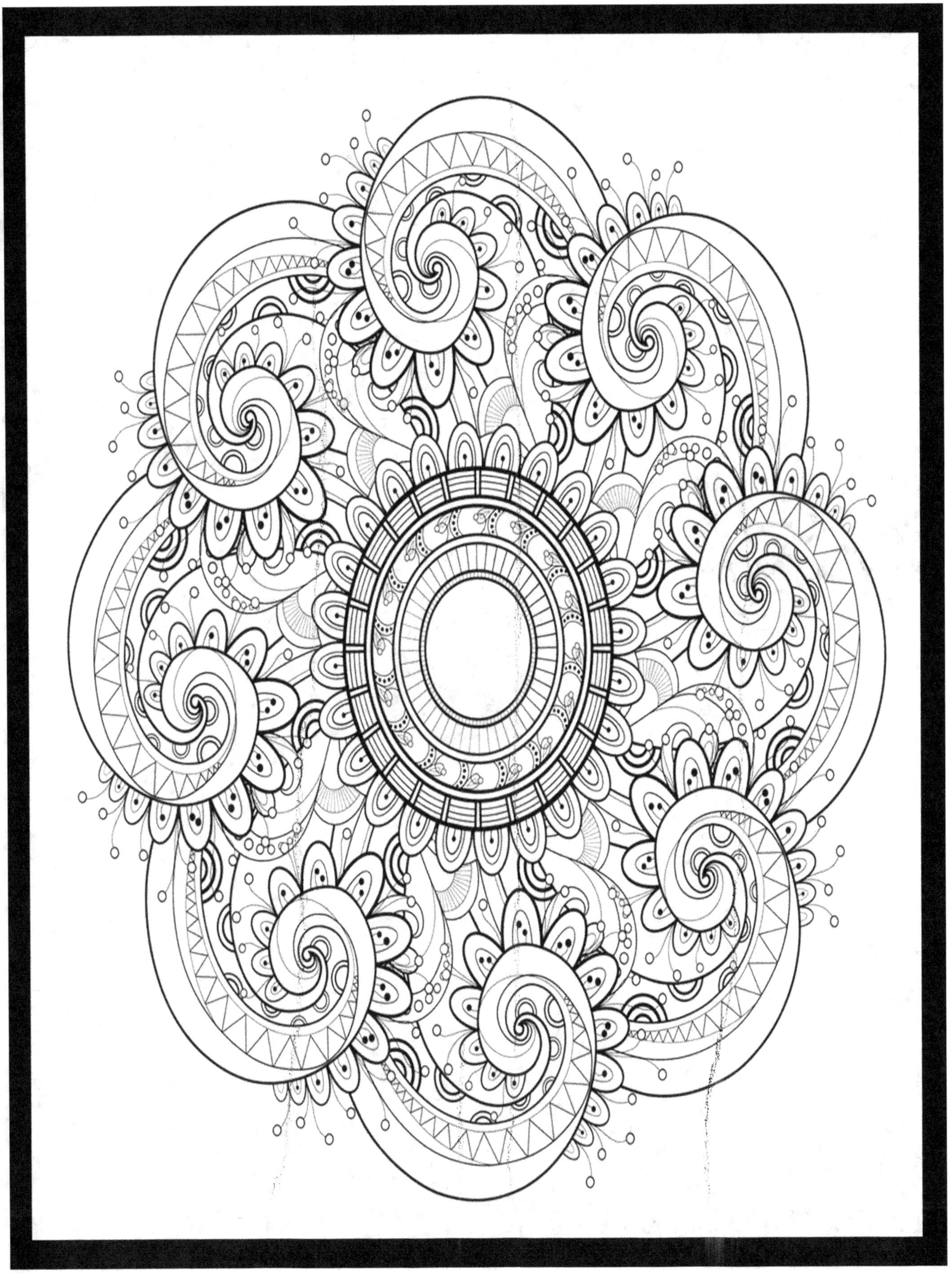

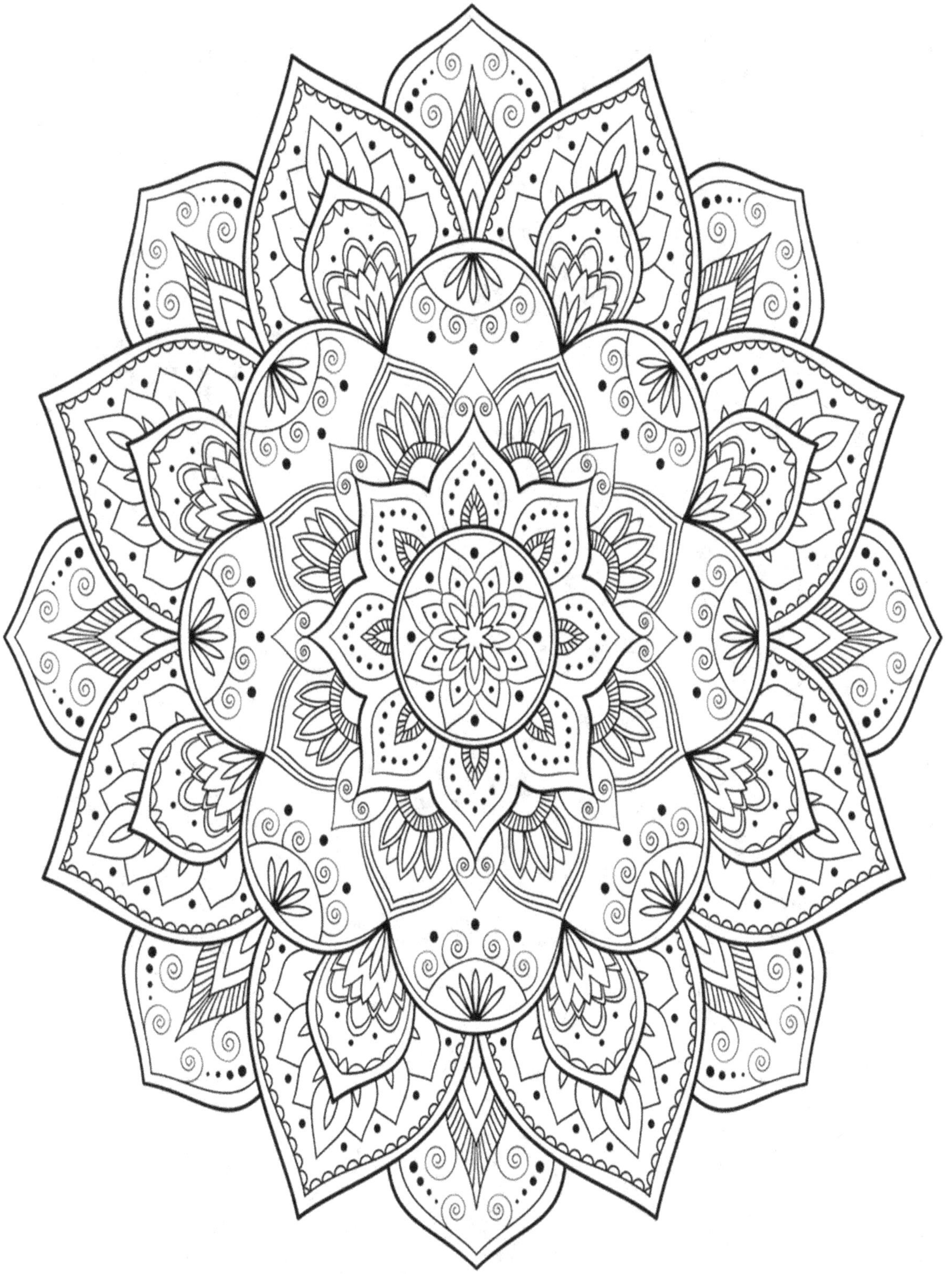

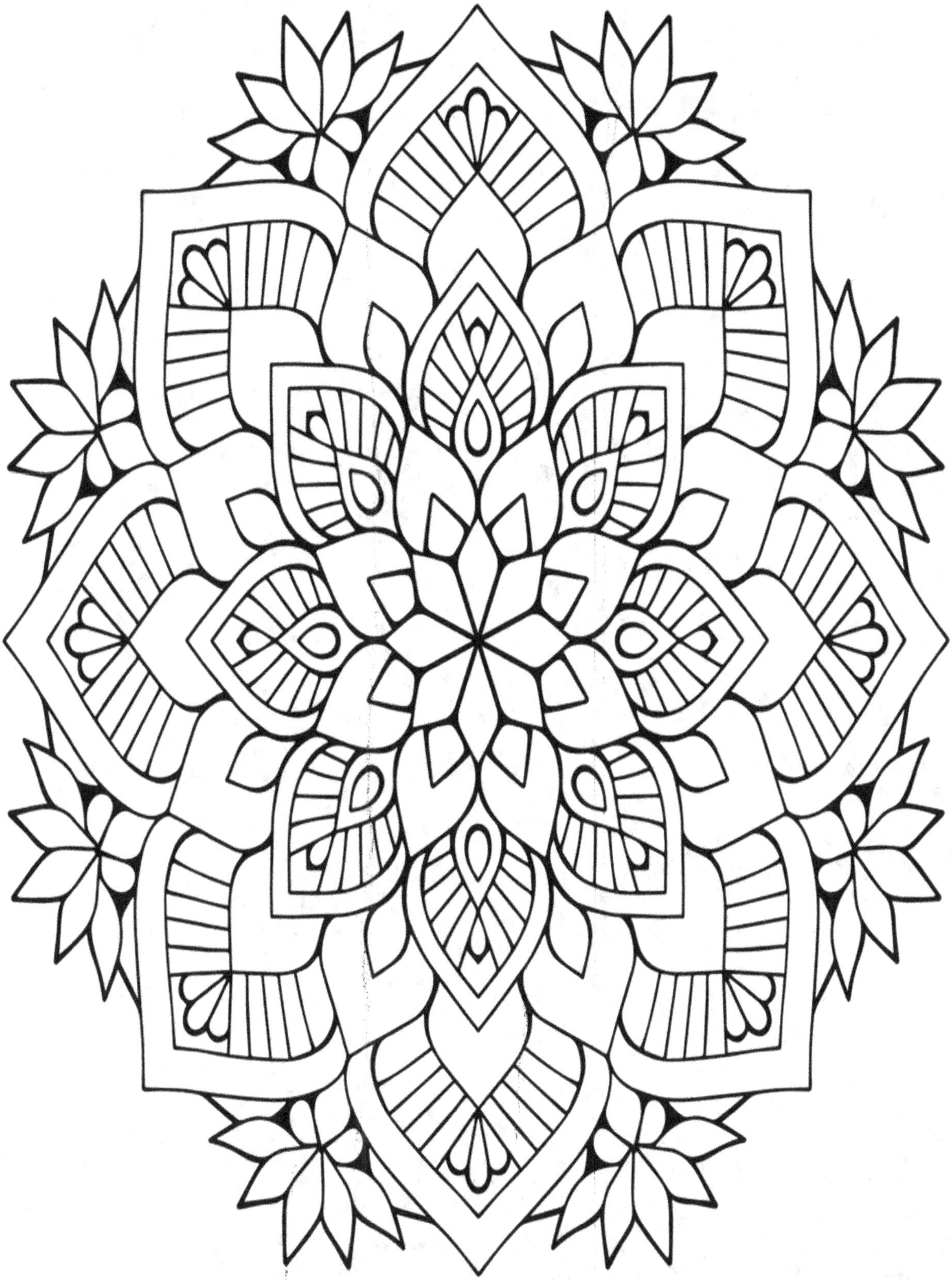

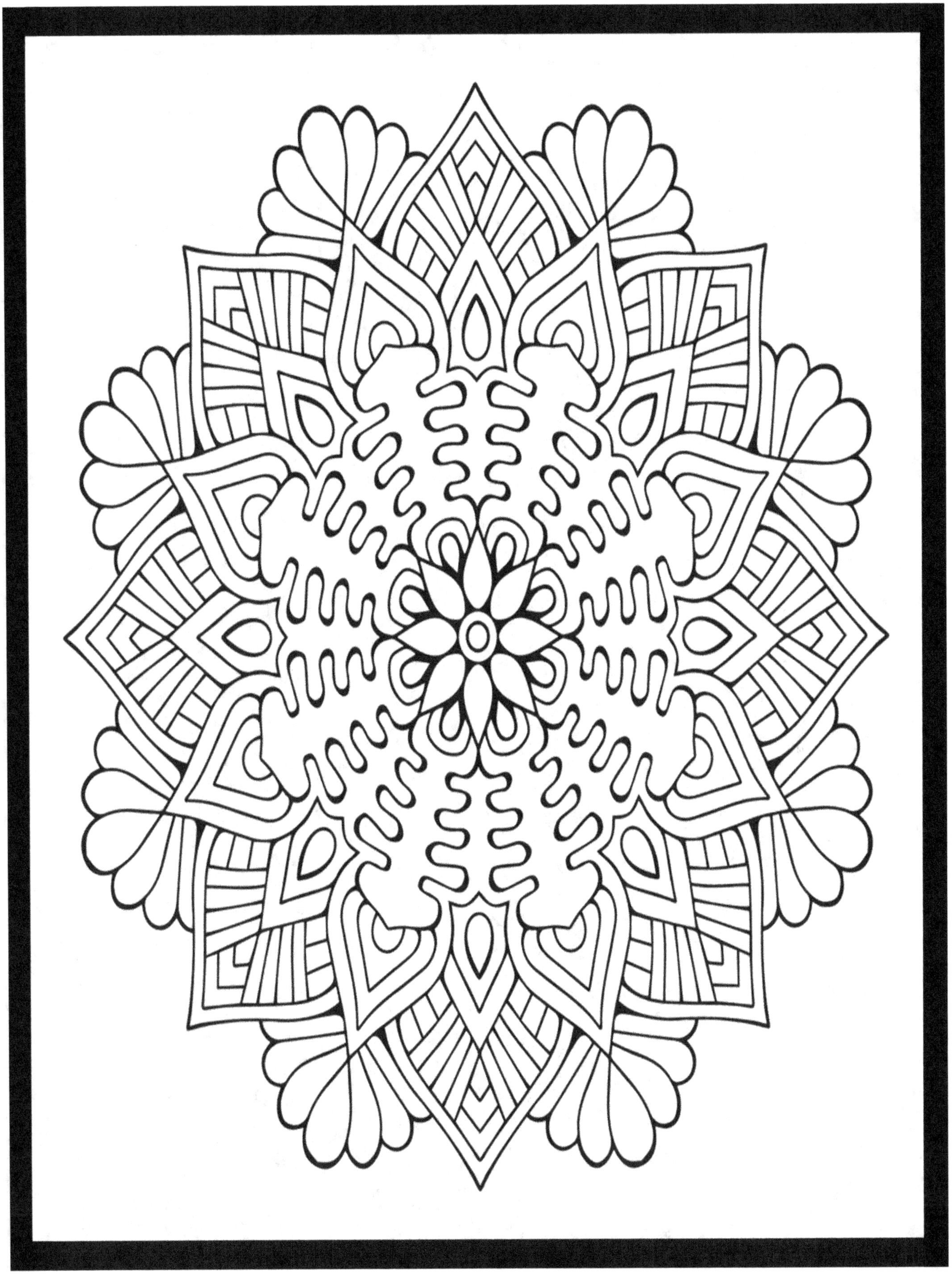

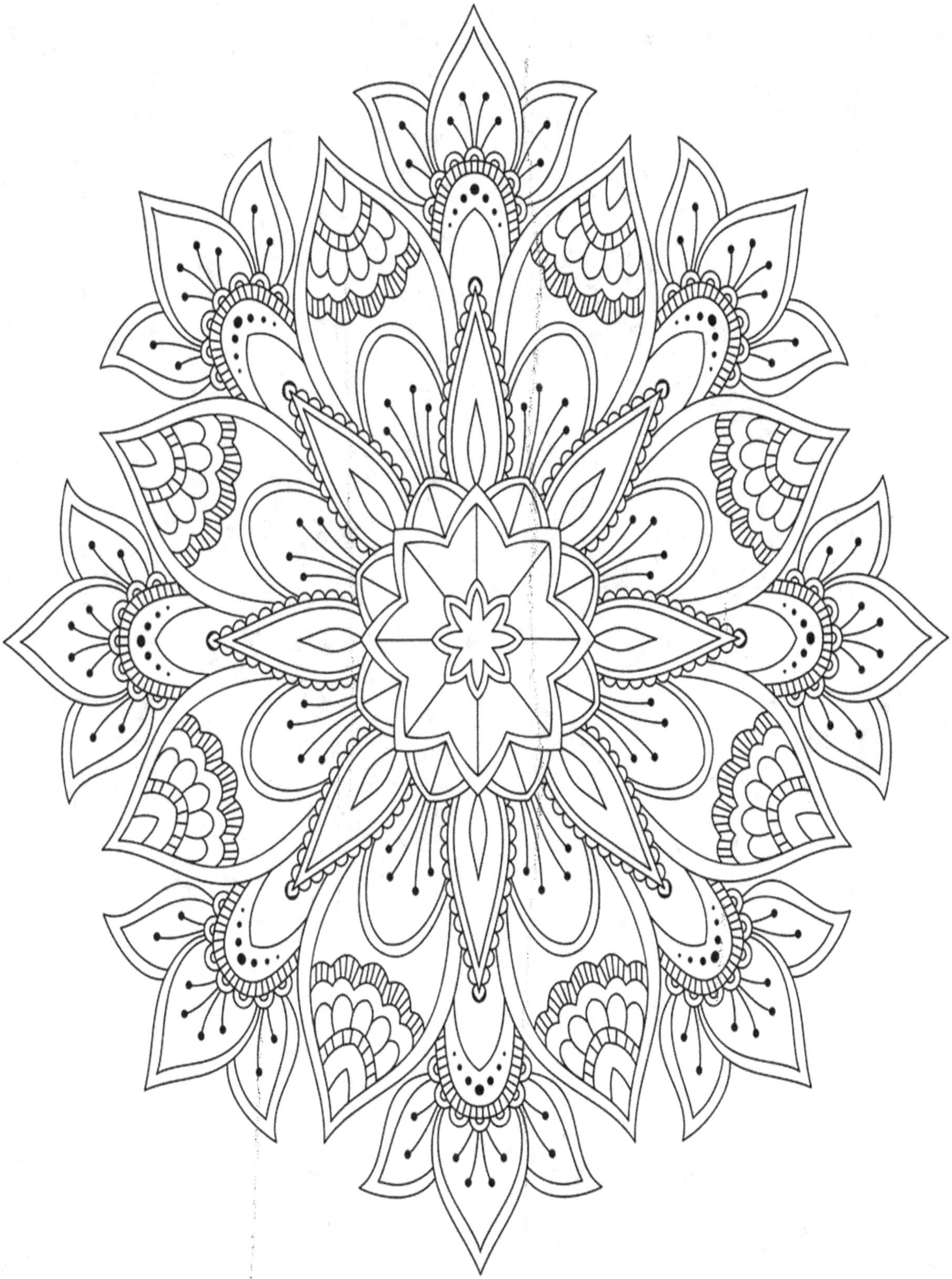

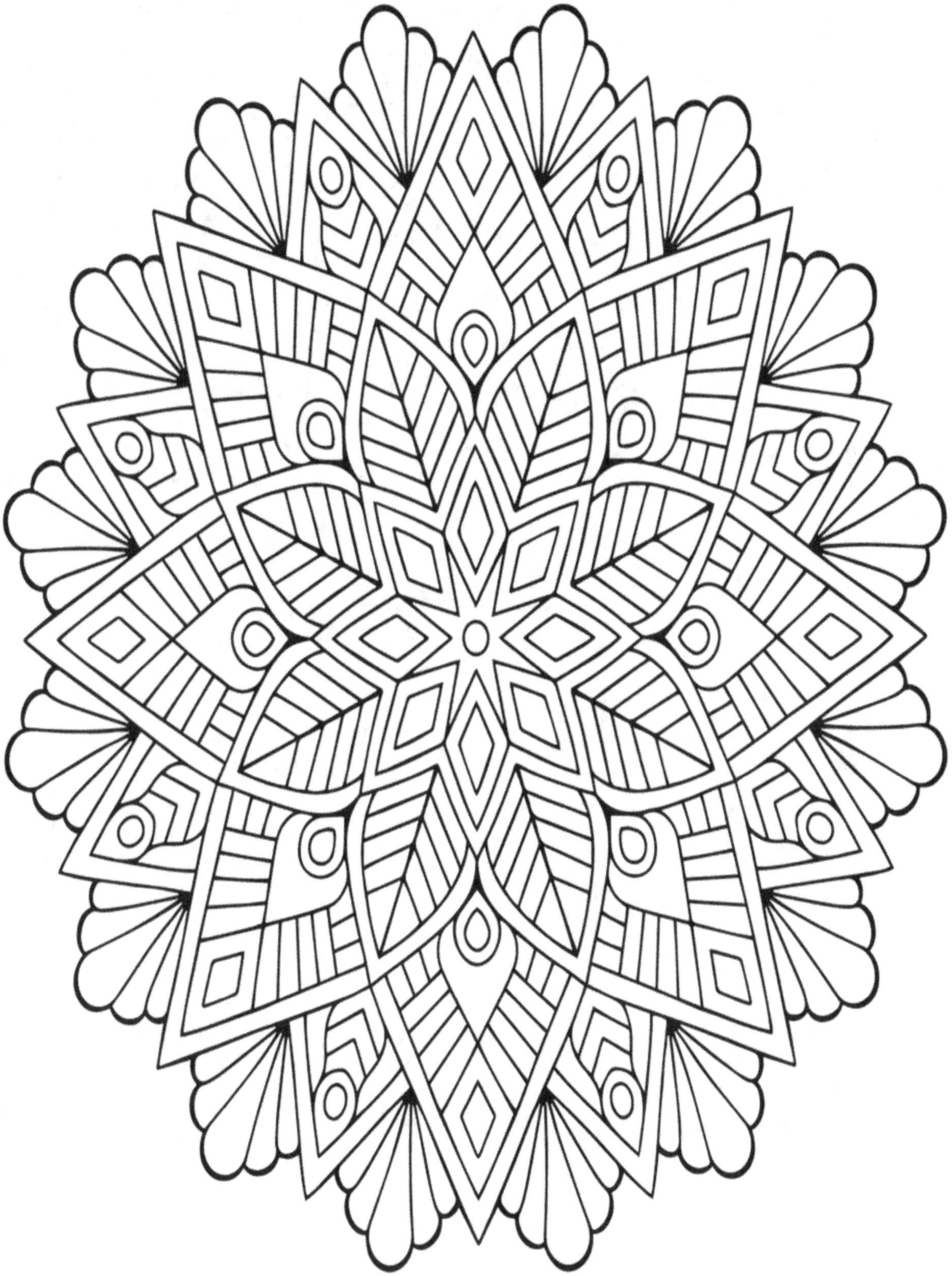

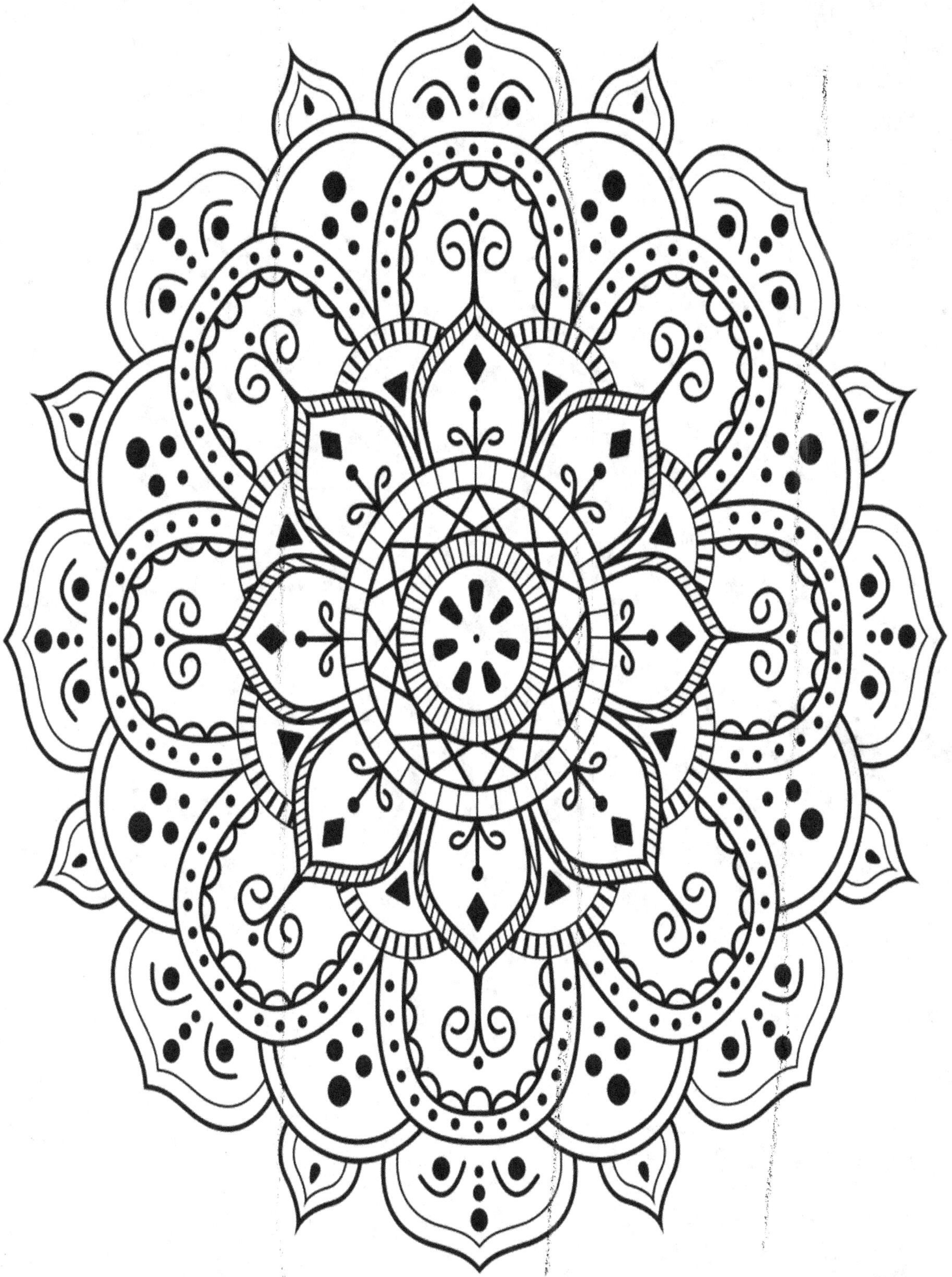

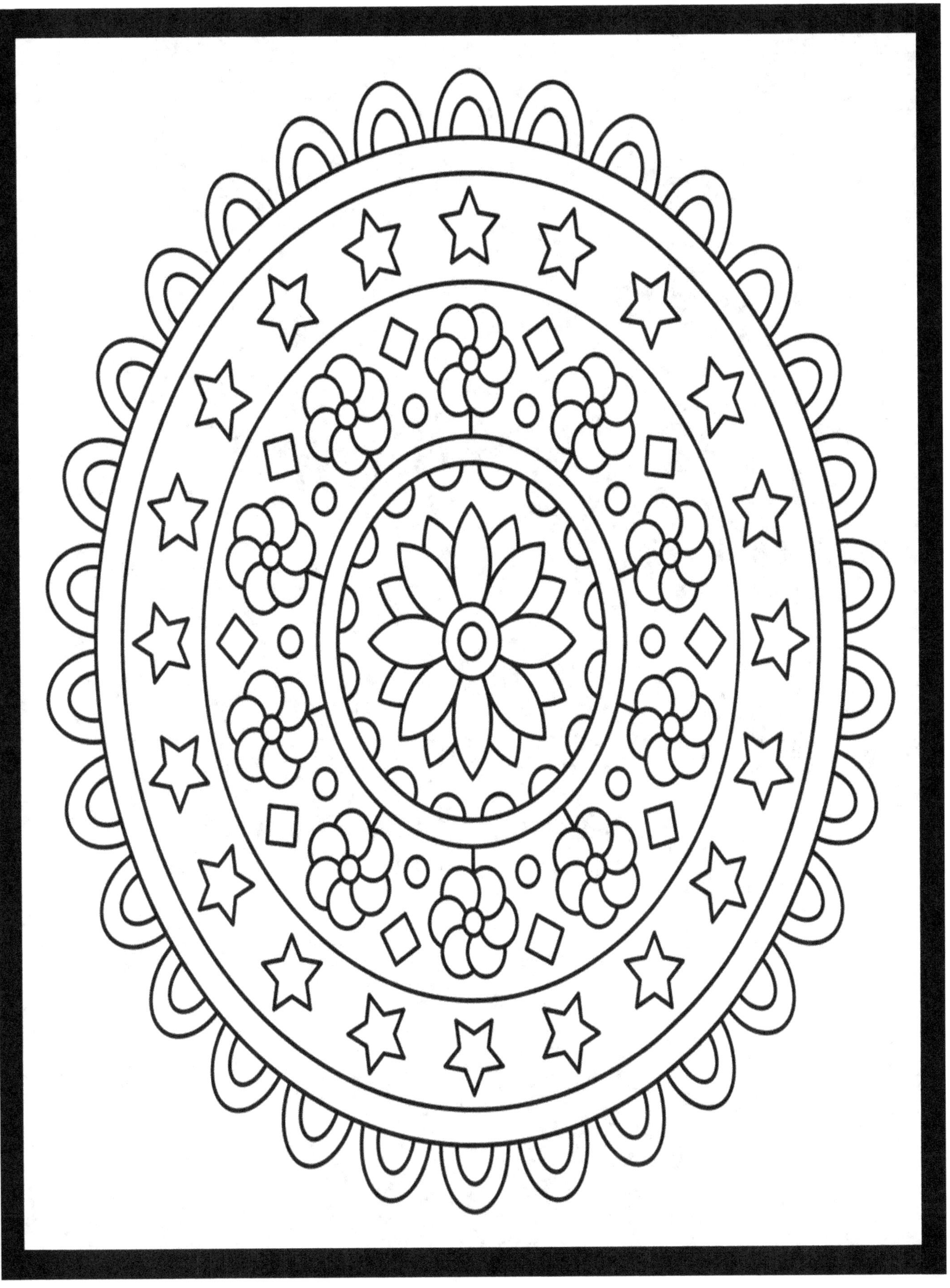

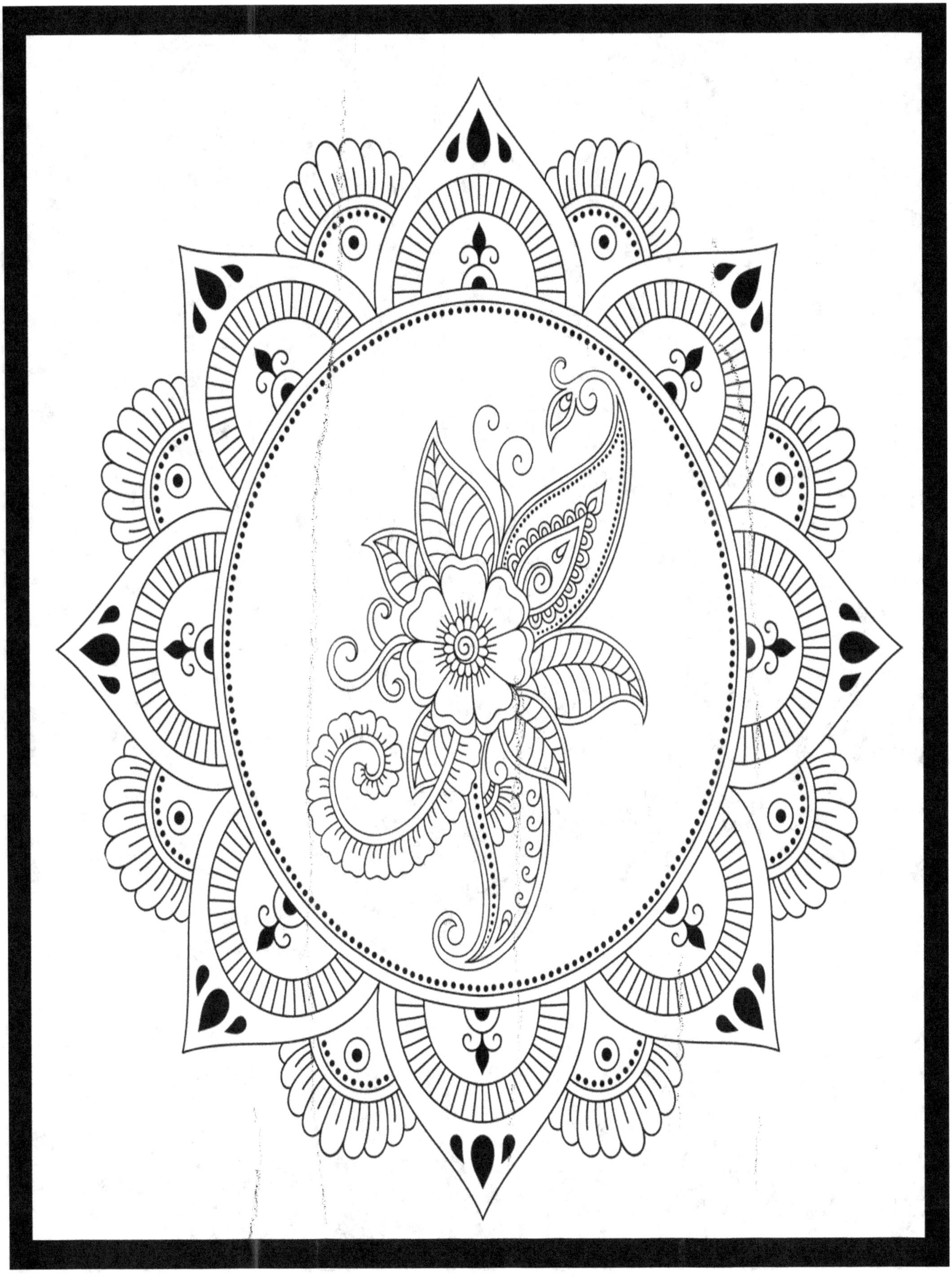

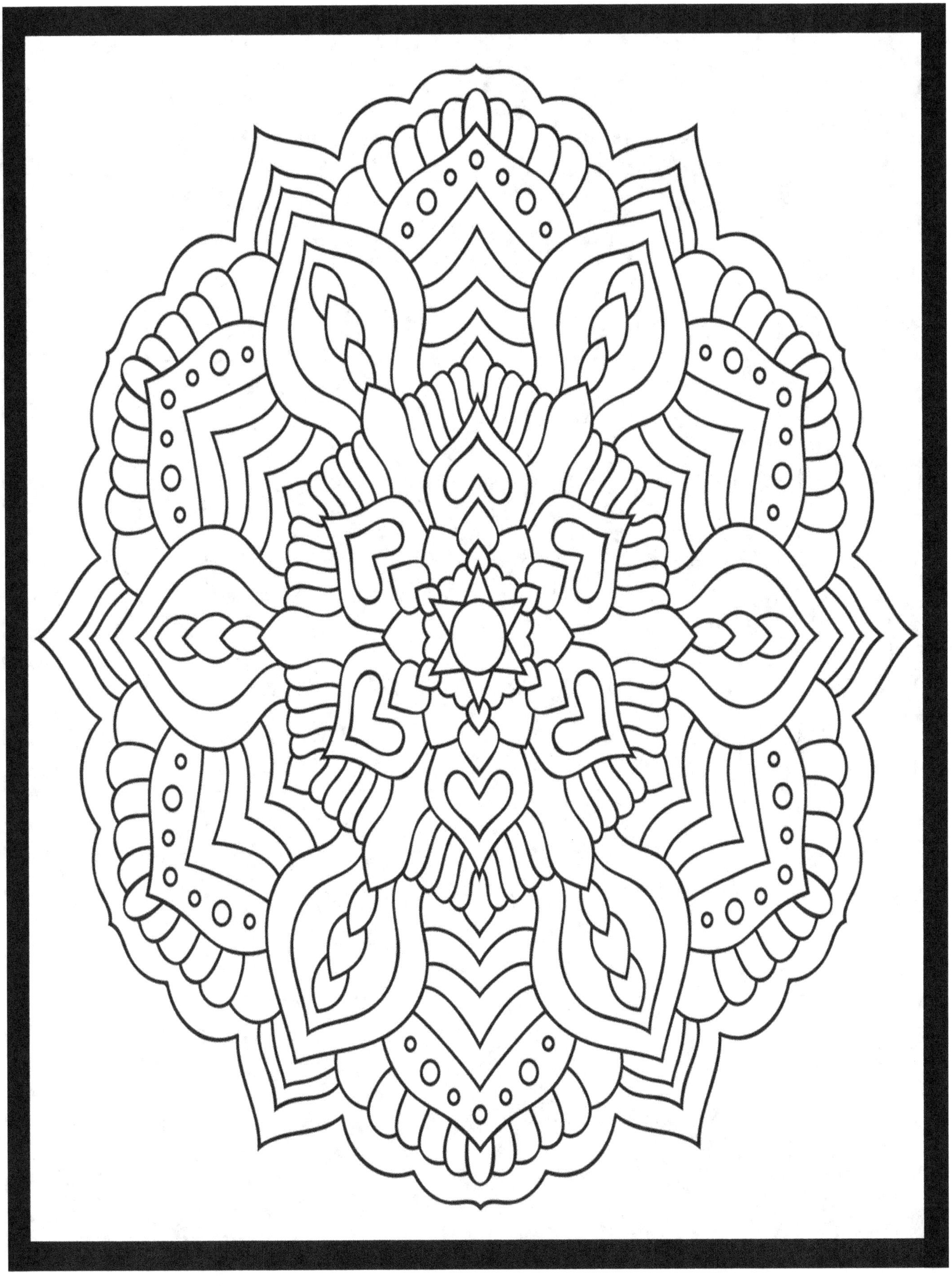

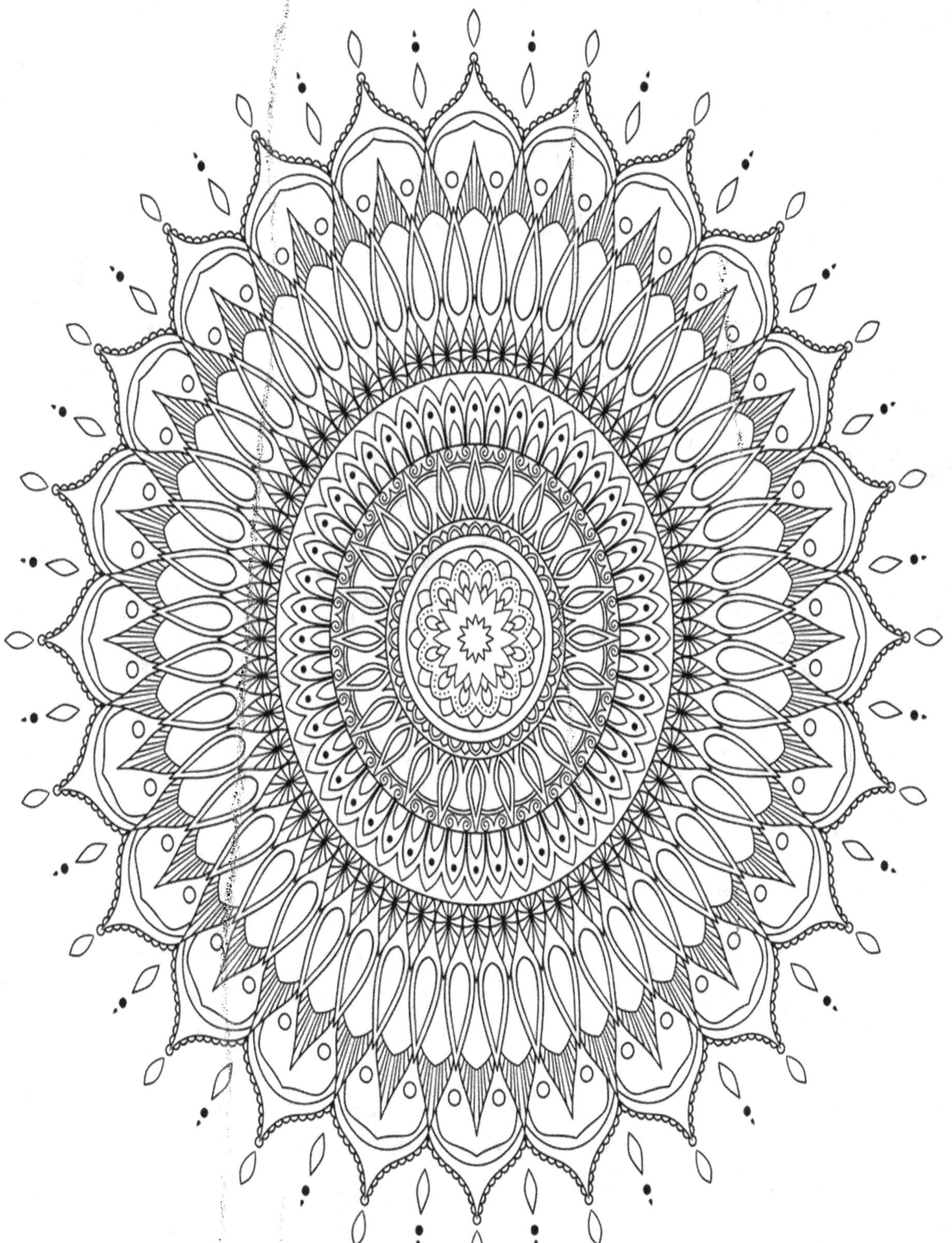

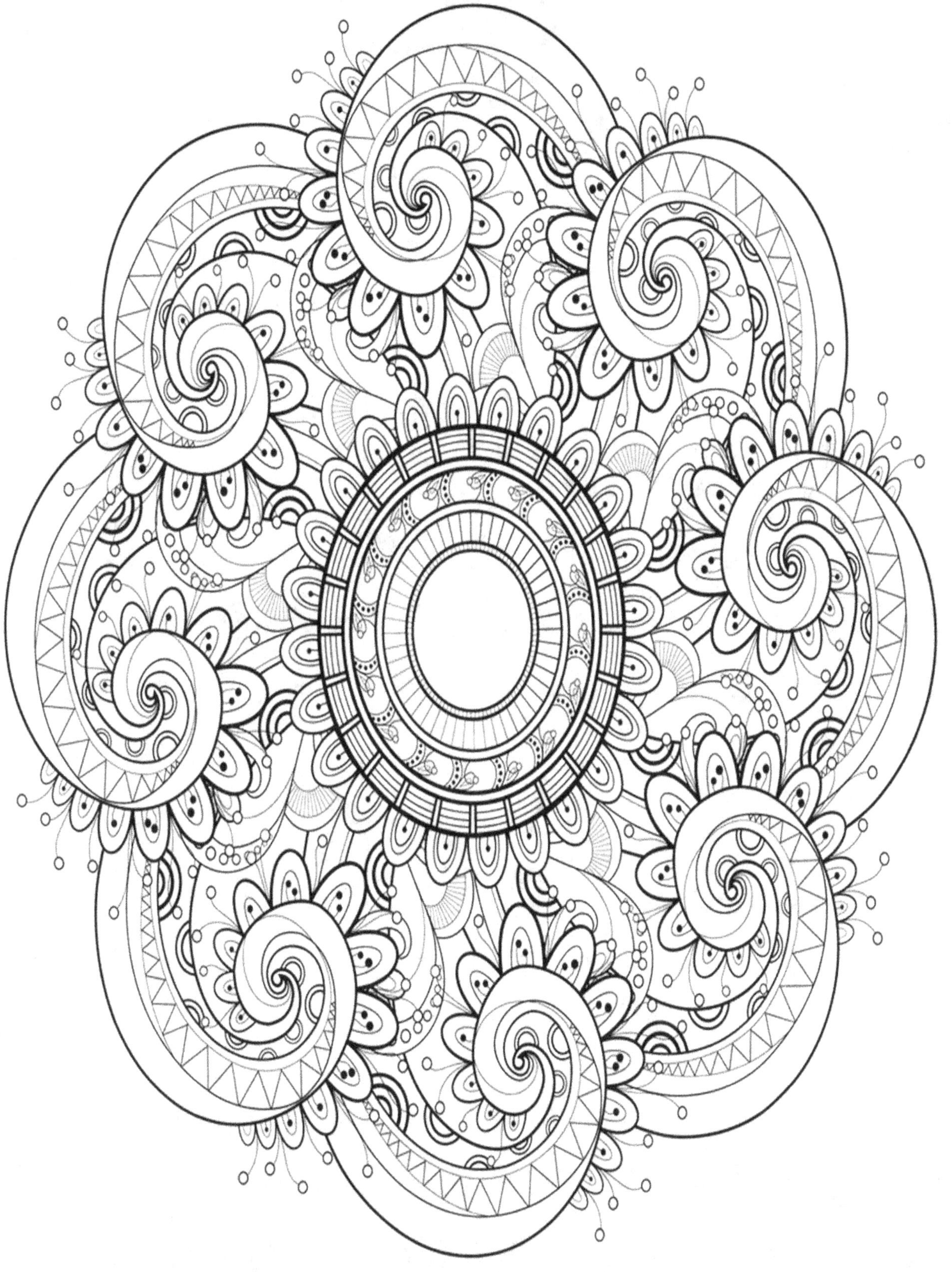

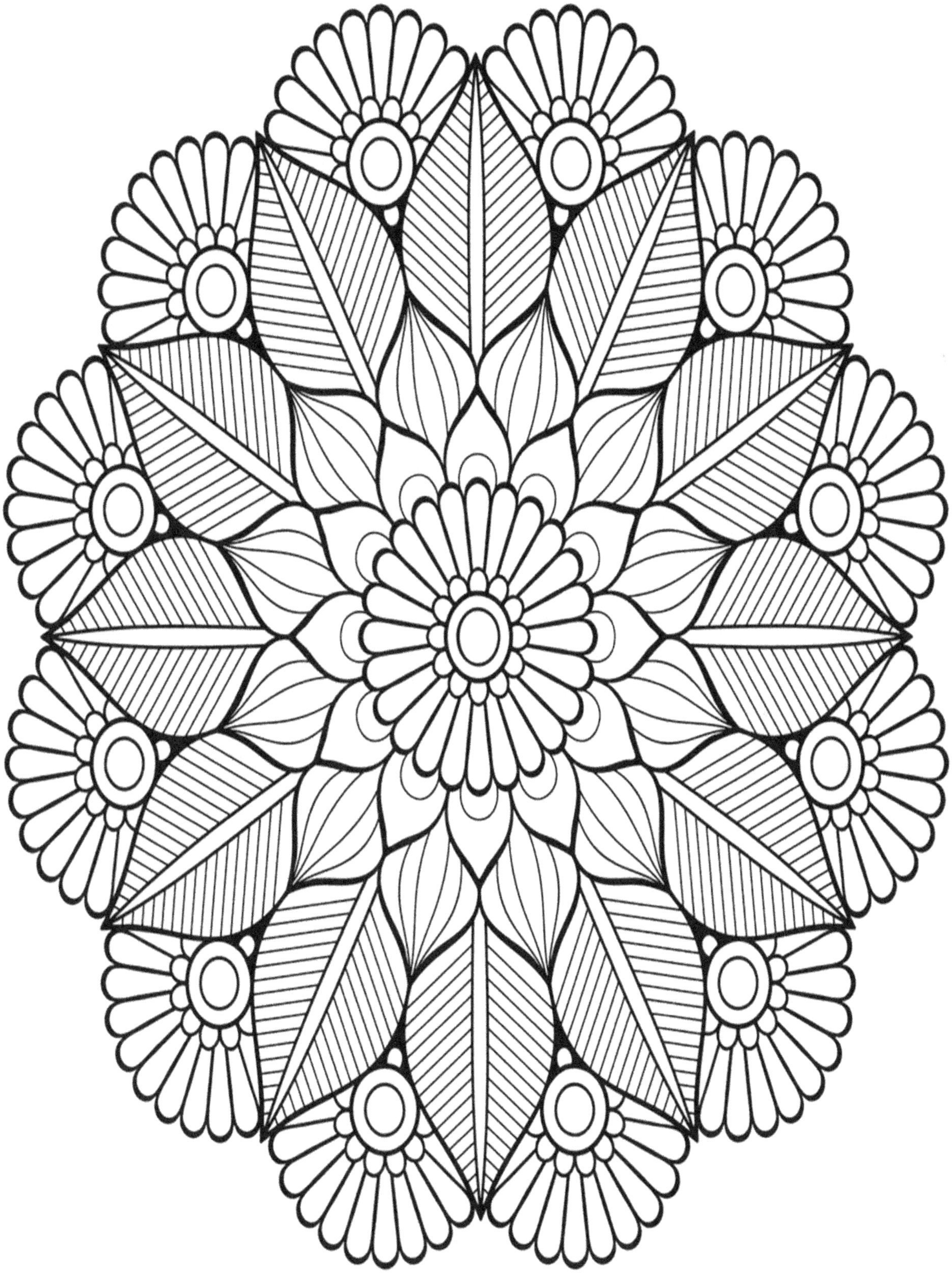

www.ingramcontent.com/pod-product-compliance
Lightning Source LLC
Chambersburg PA
CBHW080513220526
45465CB00006B/2473
9798644141401